D1198365

AT TABLE

Dueling
Chefs
A Vegetarian and
a Meat Lover
Debate the Plate

MAGGIE PLESKAC and SEAN CARMICHAEL

Amy Lynn Cheers!! MP

Amy Lynn – Enjoy!

University of Nebraska Press • Lincoln and London

Library of Congress Cataloging-in-Publication Data
  Pleskac, Maggie.
Dueling chefs : a vegetarian and a meat lover debate the plate / Maggie Pleskac and Sean Carmichael.
p. cm. — (At table series)   Includes index.
  ISBN 978-0-8032-6043-6 (pbk. : alk. paper)
1. Vegetarian cookery. 2. Cookery (Meat) 3. Cookery—Competitions. I. Carmichael, Sean. II. Title.
  TX837.P62 2007
  641.5'636—dc22   2007008285

Set in Meta by Bob Reitz. Designed by A. Shahan.

For my brother

For my moon,
my Starr,
and my son

Contents

Acknowledgments   ix

Introduction   xi

She Said

Spring   3

Summer   17

Fall   29

Winter   45

He Said

Earth   59

Water   71

Wind   83

Fire   95

Afterword   107

Weights and Measures   109

Index   111

Acknowledgments

Maggie

My special thanks go to my parents, who always stood by me, my dedicated customers and staff, who tested and tasted these vegetarian dishes at my café, and the people from the following farms, who always provided quality produce to make these pages happen: Branched Oak Farm, Shadow Brook Farm, Common Good Farm, Harvest Home Farm, Karstens Vegetable Farm, and Farmstead First Artisan Cheesemakers.

Sean

A special thanks goes to Susan Rosowski for getting the ball rolling, Rob Taylor and those at the press who guided us through the process, Lynn Hay and everyone at Chez Hay for their time and aid, Duke Ellington for *Blues in Orbit*, my family for their support and encouragement, Starr for her French toast that sustained me during late-night revisions, all the trees that made this book possible, Maggie for sticking it out, and my mom for providing me with a life of creativity and adventure in and out of the kitchen.

Introduction

Maggie

I was a waitress; he was a chef. The look on his face was priceless, or more aptly put, tasteless. I had just finished my shift and had meandered back to the kitchen to request a little lunch. Being as it was a steak and seafood restaurant, I wasn't going to be ordering off the menu. All day I had served dishes of dull, mahogany meats enhanced by the colorful vegetables on the side. That tasty color was exactly what I was after—a plate of bright grilled veggies. I approached Sean and asked if he would honor my request. He quickly responded with "Sure, no problem" and turned toward the grill with zucchini and peppers in hand. "But wait!" I blurted abruptly. "Could you grill them on a spot where no meat has touched?"

That look. I will never forget that look. It was the beginning of our ego-driven culinary competition. I had to prove to Sean that vegetarian dishes had more "meat" than even he could handle. This idea, this debate, this work in progress is a culmination of our bittersweet arguments and delicious devotion to food. Our difference of opinion is why we had to write this book together—to prove our tastes, our reasons, our passions—and to one-up the other.

This is not your typical cookbook. It is an Iron Chef duel, a sort of tit for tat, a "challenge then be challenged." In the "She Said" section, I give one of my seasonal veggie recipes to Sean, and he retaliates carnivorously with a suitable match. In the "He Said" section, Sean gives me a meaty recipe, and I have to concoct a vegetarian version. We look at each other's recipes in terms of taste, color, presentation, method of cooking, and so forth, so we're not simply mocking the same dish but rather reworking it, like directing the same play but using different leads. We exchange scripts and recast.

In "He Said" I try to find the "star" that will either look or feel the part in the recipe plot that Sean has given me. I avoid using a "double" to fit the "role," so I'm not using the many soy-meat substitutes available on the market. Soy shrimp, soy turkey, soy hot dogs, soy hamburgers, soy chicken breast, and more are available, but none of these carry any nutritional value to speak of. In my opinion, these impersonators carry too much baggage: sodium, stabilizers, and preservatives. They are also overprocessed beyond nature. I want my "lead" to shine on its own merits. I believe a vegetarian diet should center around not fleshless meats but fresh, seasonal foods that will vitalize your body, mind, and spirit.

In some of my recipes, I have cast tofu, tempeh (soy), or seitan (wheat gluten) as the meat "actors" since these ingredients are minimally processed. Tofu is made from soy milk, which is curdled and pressed into cakes in much the same way cheese is made from cow's milk. The result is a sort of custard with a texture like that of a soft, fresh cheese. Tempeh is cooked soybeans that have been pressed into cakes or patties. Tempeh's texture is chewier and more substantial than tofu's, and it has a nutty flavor. Seitan is often referred to as "wheat meat" because it is derived from wheat gluten. It has a very firm and chewy texture, making it the most meatlike substitute in the vegetable kingdom. Tofu, tempeh, and seitan all have fairly neutral flavors, making them the ideal chameleons in the kitchen, ready to take on any flavor they are given.

In "He Said" I found it easy to conquer the challenge of Sean's dishes by allowing local and fresh ingredients to spotlight my counterdish. I encourage the use of organic foods, especially for certain fruits that are more likely than others to deliver health-damaging pesticides (for example, zest of lemon rind and the delicate porous-skinned strawberry). I also often specify the use of "heirloom" fruits and vegetables. Heirloom refers to open-pollinated, nonhybrid native plants. Heirloom is to commercial produce what Grandma's home cooking is to fast food. You can taste the difference. Although many heirloom vegetables are out there, heirloom tomatoes seem to be the hot trend now, making them more available in the marketplace. I encourage you, the reader, the chef, the diner, to shop farmers' markets for high-quality, fresh, seasonal, local produce. Most farmers' markets proudly offer heirloom vegetables for their unique sizes, shapes, and colors.

One of the key ingredients in all my recipes is one that all of Sean's recipes lack—the flavor of compassion. Pure, wholesome, karma-free food from the plate to the palate. Good, clean eating with a good, clean conscience. Let the challenge begin!

Sean

I met a little girl named Maggie; I guess you could say she was . . . a vegetarian.

It was back in '97. I was working the grill at a local steak and seafood restaurant, and Maggie had just been hired as a waitress. Our debate, and in essence this book, sprang to life about an hour after we met. She asked me to grill her up some veggies, which I was more than happy to do, but then . . . she asked, "Could you please cook them on a part of the grill that hasn't been touched by meat?" The look I gave her was not one of horror but rather utter disbelief. My grill was about the size of a school desk, and the place was a high-production steak and seafood restaurant. What was she thinking? She started the cry-me-a-river clamor over cows and chickens. I, fresh out of culinary school, ranted on about how a vegetable's sole purpose was to sit and look pretty alongside my center-of-the-plate creation. The conversation was heated and ended with her refusing to eat the vegetables that I refused to make.

The debate continued, shift after shift, year after year, and within it we found common ground. Although we disagreed on what a person should eat, we did agree that it should be good. Being good means fresh, organic, awe-inspiring, and flavorful. From this common ground our friendship grew, though it was never lacking debate. She would constantly ridicule my choice of flesh, and I often told her a little pork fat would give her dishes some flavor. From this badinage came the book. The dueling swap of recipes side by side with our rib-poking, slashing-to-bits commentary is a mirror to the fellowship Maggie and I have enjoyed these many years. We have a camaraderie that has been most dear and has helped to create the chef I am today.

That being said, don't be a vegetarian if you don't have to. You're missing out on the deliciousness, the gist, the marrow of life! Literally. Look, when it comes down to it, eating in its simplest form is consuming a life to sustain your own. Whether that life comes from the field or the barn, it should be respected as such. With respect should come gratitude and with gratitude should come an elegant meal.

She Said . . .

Here are Maggie's original recipes
as presented to Sean. His recipes
are the carnivorous response to her
seasonal garden challenge.

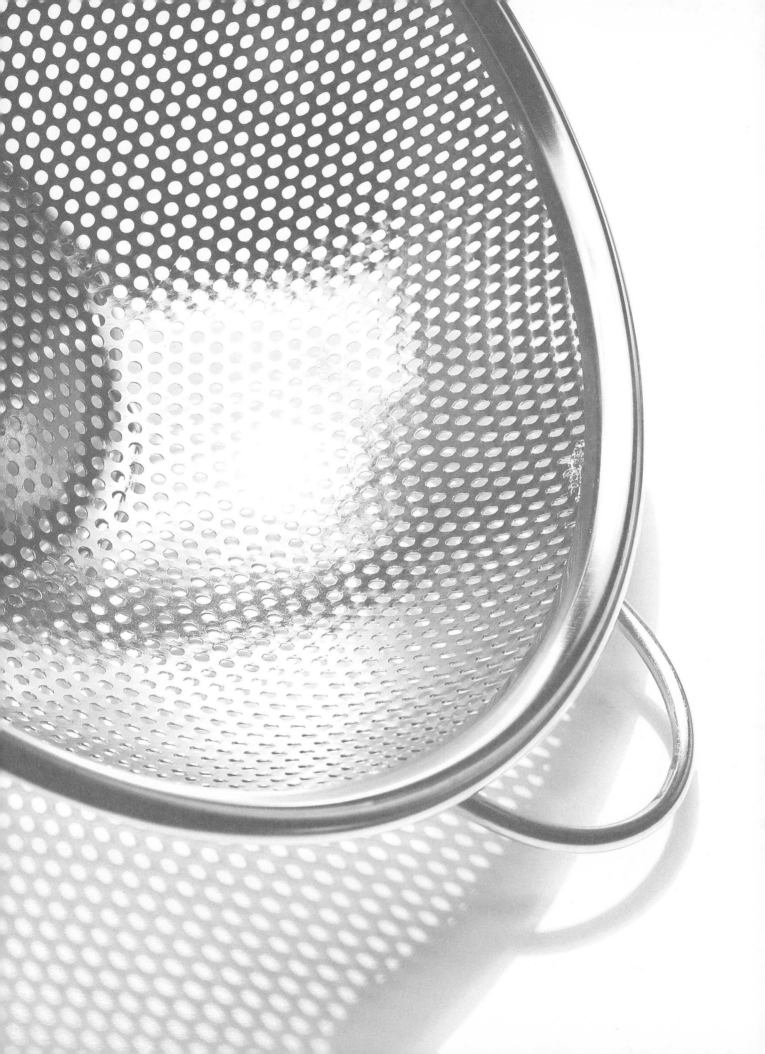

Spring

Roasted Fennel Frittata

2 pounds fennel bulbs, thinly sliced (reserve
    fronds for the custard)
10 garlic cloves, minced or pressed
2 teaspoons sea salt
2 teaspoons black pepper
3 tablespoons olive oil
10 free-range eggs, beaten

1 cup sour cream
1 cup grated Asiago cheese
1 cup chopped fresh parsley
½ cup minced fennel fronds (tops)
Sea salt
Black pepper

Preheat the oven to 375 degrees. Toss the fennel and garlic in a bowl with the salt and pepper, coating well with the olive oil. Spread evenly on a baking sheet and roast for 30 minutes or until the fennel and garlic are golden brown. Stir after the first 15 minutes to ensure even browning. Set aside to cool.

Add the sour cream to the beaten eggs and whisk until smooth. Stir in the cheese, parsley, and fennel fronds. Season lightly with salt and pepper. Add the cooled fennel and garlic mixture, including all the juices and browned bits from the baking sheet. Pour the mixture into a 9 × 13 baking pan, cover with foil, and bake in a bain-marie at 375 degrees for 1 hour or until set.

(A bain-marie, or water bath, is made by setting the baking pan inside another, larger pan filled with water halfway up the side of the baking pan.)

• •

FENNEL SEASON STARTS in the late fall and peaks in the spring. The feathery greens conjure up images of new growth and fresh tastes. The aniselike flavor is transformed by the custard and should not deter those who have an aversion to licorice flavors. Frittata is a light, protein-rich meal that can be enjoyed any time of the day — brunch, lunch, or dinner. The leftovers are excellent wrapped in a tortilla for a satisfying breakfast burrito. Sean might argue the authenticity in the preparation of my "frittata" since I have baked the dish entirely in the oven and not on a stovetop first. But Sean claims the name "strata" for a dish that traditionally includes bread as a main ingredient. So here we have successfully matched our recipes with one culinary terminology flaw to another. Not so strata, not so frittata. I think Sean should rename his recipe the Aorta Stop-a-Strata. I admit I have my share of dairy and eggs, but come on! Does he really need to invite the pig and chicken to the full yolk and cream cheese party? Carnivores who are able to sleep through their heart palpitations will be taking a long nap after his cholesterol-rich dish.

Sean

Eric-a-Strata

10 whole eggs

3 egg yolks

1½ cups milk

Kosher salt to taste

5 red potatoes, parboiled and sliced, with skins on

¼ cup (2 ounces) shredded cheddar cheese

3 ounces roasted chicken breast, cubed

3 strips bacon, cooked and chopped

2 ounces cream cheese, cubed

3 fresh basil leaves, chiffonade (sliced very thin)

One 6-ounce can artichoke hearts, drained and quartered

One 4-ounce jar roasted red peppers, sliced

1 tablespoon diced red onion

1 cup cubed sourdough bread

Preheat the oven to 375 degrees. Combine the eggs and milk in a bowl, lightly season with salt, and whisk. Line the bottom of a greased 9 × 13 casserole dish with half of the sliced potatoes. Fill with half the cheddar cheese, chicken, bacon, cream cheese, basil, artichokes, red peppers, onion, and bread cubes. Top with the remaining potato slices and pour in the egg mixture. Blanket with the remaining cheddar cheese and bake, covered with foil, for 45 minutes. Remove the foil and bake for 10 minutes or until the middle seems firm and the cheese is bubbly. Serve hot and enjoy.

· ·

TO PARBOIL POTATOES, place the washed, whole spuds in a pot of cold water on the burner at high heat. As soon as the water starts to boil, turn off the fire and let them sit for five minutes. Drain the potatoes, let them cool, and slice them as thin as you can.

One of the beauties of this egg casserole is its versatility, enabling you to use the freshest ingredients of the season or something canned from the pantry. Also, this dish will feed a large number of people with very little preparation. It can be made the day before, kept in the refrigerator overnight, and go straight from fridge to oven when needed, though you should increase the cooking time 10 to 15 minutes. Note that I have omitted pepper from the ingredients list. Pepper tends to discolor egg custards — if they are not cooked relatively quickly, they will turn a rather unappetizing shade of orange. Pepper and eggs don't really mix anyhow. If you want to add a little spice, use Tabasco sauce — it will wake up you *and* the eggs!

About this squabble over terminology that Maggie and I have enmeshed ourselves in — I say pick up a *Food Lover's Companion*, flip through, and come to your own conclusion.

All interpretations aside, you are basically getting about a day's worth of cholesterol with just one of these eggs, so you might as well throw in some bacon. You will have to walk an extra mile after either of these gratifying breakfast fête anyway, so relish the greatest savory flavor known to man, bacon.

Crustless Spinach and Mushroom Quiche

8 free-range eggs, beaten
2 pounds sour cream
1 cup finely chopped fresh parsley
2 tablespoons garlic powder
2 tablespoons onion powder
2 teaspoons dried basil
1 teaspoon sea salt

1 teaspoon black pepper
½ teaspoon ground nutmeg
1 pound chopped fresh spinach leaves
4 cups sliced mushrooms
1 cup minced scallions
1 cup shredded mozzarella cheese
1 cup shredded smoked provolone cheese

Whisk eggs and sour cream together until smooth. Whisk in parsley, garlic powder, onion powder, basil, salt, pepper, and nutmeg. Stir in the spinach, mushrooms, scallions, and cheeses. Pour into a well-oiled 9 × 13 baking pan. Cover with foil. Bake in a bain-marie at 375 degrees for 1 hour.

• •

SINCE THIS QUICHE IS SANS CRUST, I cook it in a 9 × 13 pan rather than the traditional pie shell. Sean, being culinarically correct, of course insists on a crust. I can hear him now: "How can it be a quiche without a crust?!" Well, it is. So there. If you take Sean's side and prefer a crust, simply divide the mixture into two pie shells. Crust or no crust, the most important component here is the filling. Organic, free-range eggs are a must if you want to avoid traces of steroids and antibiotics in your food. Factory farms produce unhealthy birds, which in turn produce unhealthy eggs. Buy eggs from small, local, organic farms and your quiche will show the difference. The yolks will have a brighter yellow hue, golden and healthy like sunshine. Trust me, you will taste the difference.

April showers bring more than mayflowers. Wild mushrooms crop up through the moist spring soil. For a more unique taste, check out the hand-harvested fungi available at the farmer's market. This recipe is the vernal version, but a quiche can be made with a new ingredient year-round. Use the custard ingredients as a base and substitute the season's bounty. There are 4,876,232,154 variations on a vegetarian quiche.

Sean

Lobster Quiche

Pie dough for one 9-inch pie
1 tablespoon olive oil
1½ cup coarsely chopped lobster meat
¼ cup finely diced fresh fennel
1 shallot, minced
½ cup sherry
¼ teaspoon chopped fresh dill

4 egg whites
3 whole eggs
¾ cup milk
Dash ground nutmeg
Sea salt and freshly ground pepper to taste
¼ cup (2 ounces) shredded Havarti cheese
1 tablespoon finely chopped fresh chives

Preheat the oven to 375 degrees. Place pie dough in a 9-inch pie dish, dock the bottom with a fork, and bake for 15 minutes. Heat the olive oil in a sauté pan over a medium to high flame. Add the lobster meat, fennel, and shallot, and sauté. Deglaze the pan with the sherry and reduce until almost dry. Remove from the heat and add the dill.

In a bowl lightly whip the whole eggs, egg whites, milk, nutmeg, salt, and pepper. Fill the cooled pie crust with the lobster mixture and shredded cheese. Pour the egg batter over the top and top with fresh chives. Bake for 35 to 45 minutes. Serve warm and enjoy with someone close.

• •

"DOCKING," OR PRICKING THE PIE CRUST with a fork, allows steam to escape, keeping the crust on the bottom where it should be. You can also weigh it down with uncooked beans or special ceramic beads.

Now, I don't mind naked quiches though I do prefer them with a crust. A good flaky crust is what sets the quiche apart from an everyday egg casserole. Biting through the silky custard and finishing with a satisfying crunch—heaven!

The versatility of quiche is equal to egg casserole in that your flavor combinations are limited only by your imagination and the ingredients in your pantry. They can easily be whipped together in a pinch, and the end result is more intimate and more artsy than, say, a strata. A quiche shouldn't be made the day before, at least not one with a crust, because the crust will turn out soggy. But the components can be prepared ahead of time for easy assembly.

Speaking of egg casseroles, be ever so careful when you are making Maggie's quiche; the end result could come out looking like her strata, wait, excuse me, frittata. Oh well, they are all just egg custards in a different shape anyhow. I'm not bothered by semantics. We can agree to disagree on some things.

The word "culinarically," though? And I don't know what crazy vegetarian abacus she is using to get her figure of 4,876,232,154, but slap one more bead across on my side for the lobster.

Maggie and I do agree, as always, on taste. Free-range eggs do taste the best, but their yolks still have about 213 milligrams of cholesterol each. So get rid of some of those sunshiney yolks, the two pounds of sour cream, and all that cheese, and have yourself a much healthier meal.

Curried Egg-less Salad Wrap

Four 12-inch flour tortillas
1 red onion, minced

2 heirloom tomatoes, chopped
1 head romaine lettuce, shredded

Filling

1 pound firm tofu, frozen and thawed
1 cup finely chopped fresh cilantro
1 cup Nayonnaise
8 garlic cloves, minced
2 tablespoons onion powder
2 teaspoons turmeric
2 teaspoons ground ginger

1 teaspoon ground coriander
1 teaspoon ground cumin
¼ teaspoon garam masala
½ teaspoon cayenne pepper
¼ teaspoon ground cardamom
1 teaspoon sea salt

Freeze the tofu for at least 24 hours to make sure it is frozen solid. To thaw, run under cool water or set in the refrigerator for 48 hours.

For the filling, whisk together the Nayonnaise, garlic, onion powder, turmeric, ginger, coriander, cumin, garam masala, cayenne, cardamom, and sea salt until smooth and well blended. Squeeze out all excess water from the tofu and crumble it into small pieces. Add the tofu and cilantro to the Nayonnaise mixture. Marinate in the refrigerator 4 hours or overnight.

Place half of the filling in each tortilla. Add the onions, tomatoes, and lettuce. Roll up like a burrito, folding the sides inward while keeping the filling enclosed. Cut in half on a diagonal. Prop one half upright against the other for an attractive presentation.

· ·

IN BOTH APPEARANCE AND TEXTURE this reminds me of an egg salad with curry except that it's entirely vegan (no dairy, no egg). Nayonnaise is a vegan mayonnaise made by Nasoya; it can be found at most natural foods stores. If you can't find Nayonnaise, you could substitute mayonnaise, but then it wouldn't be vegan (mayonnaise is made with egg). Freezing and thawing the tofu is crucial since this process creates a porous texture that allows the tofu to soak up the sauce. It makes this recipe a little more involved and requires a bit more planning, but it's well worth it.

Sean

Gingered Bison Lettuce Wraps with a Cold Ginger Sauce

1 pound ground American bison
1 small yellow onion, finely diced
2 garlic cloves, minced
½ cup minced fresh ginger
1 tablespoon sambal oelek
Kosher salt and freshly ground black pepper to taste
1 tablespoon molasses

2 tablespoons hoisin
1 large head romaine lettuce
1 carrot, shredded
1 daikon, julienned
1 cucumber, peeled, seeded, and julienned
1 cup shredded white cabbage
1 cup chopped fresh cilantro
¼ cup freshly squeezed lime juice

In a wok or skillet, brown the ground bison over medium to high heat. Drain the excess juices, return to the heat, and add the onions, garlic, ginger, sambal oelek, salt, and pepper. Stir to incorporate these ingredients and reduce the heat to medium low. Cook until the onions are translucent. Mix in the molasses and hoisin and remove from the heat. Transfer to a bowl and reserve.

Cut the bottom stalk off of the romaine lettuce and discard. Remove, wash, and dry the larger outer leaves. Fill the bottom half of each leaf with the desired amount of the cooked meat mixture, carrot, daikon, cucumber, cabbage, and cilantro. Carefully roll up the filled leaf to the top and place on a plate or platter to serve. Drizzle the lime juice over each rolled wrap and serve with cold ginger sauce. Enjoy as never before.

Cold Ginger Sauce

1 tablespoon peeled fresh ginger
¾ cup dark honey
½ cup soy sauce

½ cup cane vinegar
1 teaspoon sambal oelek
¼ cup finely chopped scallions

Combine the fresh ginger, honey, soy sauce, and vinegar in a food processor and pulse until well incorporated. Transfer to a serving bowl and add the scallions on top.

· ·

WHY ARE VEGETARIANS obsessed with wraps? Wraps have become the new salads. They wrap everything in all different colors and flavors of tortilla. It's almost as if they don't want to see what they are eating, which if you peruse the meat-substitute aisle of your local market, is probably the case. You shouldn't fear your food.

Sambals are condiments stemming from Indonesia and Malaysia. Sambal oelek is made with a mixture of chili peppers, brown sugar, and salt. Hoisin is a deep brown sauce made from soybeans, garlic, chili peppers, and various spices that is used as a condiment in addition to flavoring many Chinese dishes. Both will increase the fire factor in your dish, so they should be used accordingly with your temperament.

The daikon is an Asian radish that has a sweet, juicy, white flesh and adds a fresh crispness to the plate when used raw. All these ingredients, including the cane vinegar, fresh ginger, and dark honey, can be purchased at an Asian market if they are unavailable at your local supermarket.

Bison is a wonderfully flavorful meat that has added health benefits. Its rich, almost sweet, flavor is like that of choice beef and not at all gamy as some would expect.

Bison is a naturally tender lean meat that is handled as little as possible. The animals themselves live entirely on grass, as they have for ages, and are not subjected to controversial drug and hormone treatments. Bison is a great source of iron and vitamin B-12. It also contains less fat and cholesterol than salmon, pork, chicken, or beef. If you are having a hard time finding bison, contact the National Bison Association and they can point you to a local retailer.

In this recipe I julienne the radish and cucumber, though they both could be shredded like the carrot and cabbage if time doesn't allow. To julienne is to cut food, generally fruits and vegetables, into thin matchstick strips. In this recipe you would begin by peeling the daikon, then cutting a strip off one side to form a flat bottom to prevent the daikon from rolling and causing yourself bodily injury. Cautiously, with a very sharp knife, slice the radish lengthwise into ⅛-inch strips. Stack these strips on top of each other, five strips high. Finally, and just as cautiously, slice each stack lengthwise into ⅛-inch sticks.

Although in this recipe I tabled the final dish as wraps rolled full of ingredients, you could serve it with the components separated, allowing your guests to mix and match to their liking.

Avocado Melt with Herb-Mustard Dressing

4 slices French or sourdough bread, thickly
    sliced and toasted
2 avocados
2 heirloom tomatoes, sliced
1 red onion, minced

½ cup roasted sunflower seeds
¾ cup shredded smoked provolone cheese
¾ cup shredded mild cheddar cheese
¾ cup shredded mozzarella cheese
One 2-ounce bag of alfalfa sprouts

Herb-Mustard Dressing

½ cup mayonnaise
¼ cup prepared yellow mustard
1 tablespoon soy sauce
2 teaspoons onion powder

1 teaspoon garlic powder
½ teaspoon dried thyme
¼ teaspoon dried dill
¼ teaspoon dried basil

Set oven to broil. For the dressing, combine mayonnaise, mustard, soy sauce, onion powder, garlic powder, thyme, dill weed, and basil and whisk until well blended. Spread dressing heavily on the toasted bread. Cut the avocados in half and remove the seed. Using a spoon, carefully scoop out the flesh from each half. Cut the flesh in thin slices. Layer the avocado slices, tomato slices, onion, sunflower seeds, and cheeses on each of the 4 slices of bread. Place under a broiler for 3 minutes or until cheeses are well melted and beginning to brown. Top with additional dressing and alfalfa sprouts and serve open-faced.

. . . .

AVOCADOS GET A BAD RAP for their fat content. While it's true they are high in unsaturated fat, half of an 8-ounce avocado weighs in at just 138 calories. The buttery avocado is rich in potassium and vitamin E. There are two common varieties, each with distinct color and skin textures. The Hass variety is black with a rough surface and the Fuerte is green and smooth. I made this recipe in a tortilla wrap at my café and it was the best seller among nonvegetarians. The open-faced sandwich makes a nice presentation on the plate. If you have tortillas on hand, try it wrapped up for a convenient lunch on the go.

Sean

Smoked Halibut on Ciabbata with Fried Avocado Slices and Roasted Yellow Pepper Crème Fraîche

8 slices ciabbata
1 cup peanut oil
3 avocados
1 cup panko (Japanese-style dry bread crumbs)
⅔ cup (4 ounces) mung bean sprouts

4 slices Manchego cheese
1 pound smoked halibut
3 tablespoons capers, drained and washed
2 tablespoons very thinly sliced red onion

Toast the ciabbata slices in a 350-degree oven until lightly browned. Heat the peanut oil in a saucepan. Peel and slice the avocados into ¼-inch wedges. Dredge the avocado wedges in the panko and lightly fry in the oil until golden. Gently remove with a slotted spoon and drain on paper towels.

Divide the mung bean sprouts between the plates and top with two slices of bread. Place the cheese slices on top of the bread and then layer with the halibut. Sprinkle with capers and onions and drizzle with crème fraîche. Enjoy the love.

Roasted Yellow Pepper Crème Fraîche

2 yellow bell peppers
1 teaspoon olive oil
1 garlic clove
3 fresh basil leaves

½ teaspoon unsweetened grapefruit juice
¼ cup sour cream
½ teaspoon lemon juice
Pinch of salt

Coat the yellow peppers with the olive oil. Set the peppers over an open flame such as a gas burner, grill, or the broiler of the oven. Carefully, and with tongs, continually turn the peppers until the outer skin is completely charred. Transfer the peppers to a small mixing bowl and seal the top with plastic wrap. Allow the peppers to sweat in the bowl until they are cool enough to handle. Using a paring knife, remove and discard the charred skin, stems, and seeds. Cut the remaining pepper flesh into eighths. In a food processor chop the garlic and fresh basil. Add the roasted yellow peppers and grapefruit juice and purée until smooth. Add the sour cream and lemon juice and blend until the sour cream and peppers are well incorporated and smooth. Can be kept refrigerated in a sealed container for up to a week.

• • • • • • • • • • • • • • • • • • • •

IF TIME OR RESOURCES ELUDE YOU, substitute ½ cup canned roasted yellow peppers for the freshly roasted peppers. Also, I am cheating a little on the crème fraîche, but if you have the time and resources, you can make your own. Combine 2 tablespoons of buttermilk with 1 cup of heavy whipping cream in a glass jar. Cover and let stand at room temperature for one day. Stir before using and refrigerate.

This sandwich has the benefit of a light yet satisfying lunch or dinner. The smokiness of the fish works well with the silkiness of the crème fraîche, and the creamy crunch of the fried avocados is augmented by the fresh bean sprouts. When buying mung bean sprouts, be sure to pick crisp, fresh-looking sprouts with the buds still attached; avoid the slimy or off-smelling sprouts. By the way, it's okay to eat meat *and* bean sprouts. You don't have to limit yourself like a vegetarian.

Maggie

Golden Crepes with Goat Cheese, Spinach, and Strawberries

Crepe Batter

2 free-range eggs, beaten
1 cup organic unbleached flour
1½ cup organic milk or soy milk
1 tablespoon olive oil

1 teaspoon turmeric
1 teaspoon sea salt
¼ teaspoon ground cumin
¼ teaspoon ground coriander

Filling

8 ounces chèvre cheese
1 pound fresh spinach, lightly steamed

1 cup toasted pine nuts
1 pint fresh organic strawberries, sliced

In a bowl, blend all batter ingredients with an electric mixer or whisk. Heat a 10-inch nonstick skillet over medium to high heat. Remove the skillet from the heat. Hold the skillet in one hand, and with the other hand spoon in ¼ cup of the batter. Rotate the skillet around to spread the batter, covering the bottom in a thin, even layer. Return the skillet to the heat for 45 to 60 seconds or until the crepe is lightly browned. Invert the pan and, using a spatula, drop the crepe onto a paper towel. Repeat with remaining batter. Spread chèvre on the unbrowned side of the crepe. Layer on steamed spinach and toasted pine nuts. Roll up like a jelly roll or fold into quarters. Top with sliced strawberries.

• •

I CAME UPON THIS COMBINATION of flavors by accident during a farm tour. The farmers were offering edible samples that had been harvested on site. The tasting table included fresh chèvre (a soft goat cheese) rolled in curry powder, a jar of strawberry preserves, and a large basket of fresh-picked spring greens. Because the plates were small, I loaded these delights on without much room for separation. Toward my last few bites they had commingled into one amazing flavor. I closed my eyes, sat back, chewed slowly, swallowed, and sighed gratefully. This recipe is my attempt to incorporate all those separate flavors into that one memorable bite.

Sean

Mediatrice Crepes (Peacekeeping Crepes)

Crepe Batter

¾ cup all-purpose flour
3 large eggs, slightly beaten
½ cup whole milk
¼ cup flat beer (any domestic ale)

Pinch salt
Pinch Old Bay seasoning
6 teaspoon melted butter

Whisk together the flour, eggs, milk, beer, salt, Old Bay seasoning, and 4½ teaspoons of the butter to form a smooth, thin batter. Refrigerate for at least 1 hour before continuing. Prepare the filling in the interim. Heat a crepe pan over a medium to high flame. After it is hot, brush the whole pan with a light coating of the remaining butter. Ladle ¼ cup of the batter into the bottom of the pan and at the same time tilt the pan so the batter evenly coats the whole pan. Cook for about 2 minutes, or until the bottom starts to brown and the top looks dry. Using a rubber spatula, carefully turn the crepe over and cook for 30 seconds more. Transfer to a plate and cover loosely with parchment paper. Continue with the process until the batter is used up or until you have made the desired number of crepes.

Crepe Filling

1 garlic clove, minced
2 teaspoons truffle oil
16 bluepoint oysters, shucked and drained
1 teaspoon onion powder
½ teaspoon Old Bay seasoning
Pinch freshly ground nutmeg
½ cup heavy whipping cream

2 tablespoons sour cream
Kosher salt and freshly ground black pepper to
    taste
½ pound fresh baby spinach
2 tablespoons minced cornichons
2 tablespoons minced red onion
1 diced beefsteak tomato

In a medium saucepan over medium heat, sauté the minced garlic in 1 teaspoon of the truffle oil for about 1 minute. Add the oysters, onion powder, Old Bay seasoning, and nutmeg, and sauté for 2 more minutes. Stir in the whipping cream and sour cream, season with salt and pepper, and simmer for 5 minutes. Take the pan off the heat and let cool slightly. Stir in the spinach, cornichons, red onion, and tomato. Spoon 2 oysters with some of its sauce on one edge of a crepe and carefully roll up tight. Place rolled crepes on a plate and drizzle the remaining teaspoon of truffle oil over the top. Serve warm and enjoy the peace.

• •

I CAME UPON THIS COMBINATION of flavors on purpose during a hurly-burly tour of the Big Easy inspired by my love of the po' boy sandwich. These crepes, like the grand master of all sandwiches, are a fantastic dish for a special night when the aphrodisiac qualities of the oysters are sought. They can also help in quelling an angry mate when you come in late.

Fresh oysters should be plump and uniform in size, smell fresh, and have good color. With advancements in technology and refrigeration you don't have to worry about eating fresh oysters only in months that end with an "r." They do, however, taste better in the fall and winter months. During the summer months they spawn and become soft and fatty. The most important rule with oysters is "The earlier they're eaten, the finer the flavor."

Crepe pans are shallow with sloping sides and a flat bottom and are usually coated with a nonstick finish. A good pan will go a long way toward making a good crepe, but do not despair if your crepes aren't coming out perfect. I know a number of chefs who have a hard time flipping a crepe without breaking it.

Summer

Falafel Burger with Tahini-Mint Dressing

Burger Patties

2 cups garbanzo beans, cooked or canned
¼ cup bulgur wheat, soaked in ¼ cup hot water until water is absorbed
¾ cup minced onion
2 tablespoons minced garlic
¼ cup fresh parsley
¼ cup fresh cilantro
¼ cup water

1 tablespoon cumin seed
2 teaspoons coriander seed
1 teaspoon sea salt
1 teaspoon black pepper
1 teaspoon baking powder
½ teaspoon turmeric
¼ teaspoon cayenne pepper
4 sesame buns, toasted

Combine all ingredients except sesame buns in a food processor and blend well 5 to 10 minutes. Transfer mixture to a bowl, cover and refrigerate overnight. Form falafel mixture into burger-size patties.

To bake: Spray or oil a baking sheet and bake at 375 degrees for 30 to 35 minutes. Flip sides after first 15 minutes.

To fry: Heat the oil in a skillet and fry until both sides are golden and encrusted

Tahini-Mint Dressing

1 cucumber, peeled and seeded
½ cup tahini
¼ cup lemon juice
¼ cup fresh mint or 2 tablespoons dried mint

1 tablespoon fresh parsley
1 tablespoon fresh cilantro
1 teaspoon sea salt

Combine all ingredients in a food processor and blend until smooth and creamy. Add water to thin consistency.

Toppings

2 heirloom tomatoes, sliced
1 cucumber, sliced

1 red onion, sliced
Shredded lettuce

Serve burger patties on toasted sesame buns and top with dressing and veggie condiments

. . . .

TRADITIONALLY, THIS MIDDLE EASTERN DISH is formed into balls or croquettes and served on pita, but my version is formed into a burger patty and served on a bun. The sesame-flavored buns are a must for their outstanding toasted flavor and their pairing with the spicy falafel and sesame dressing. Tahini, an ingredient in the dressing, is a thick paste of ground sesame seeds that is similar in texture to peanut butter. It can be found at health food stores and at Middle Eastern and Asian markets. It is the main ingredient in hummus and baba ganoush and is an excellent dairy substitute for creamy-style sauces. If tahini is unavailable, you could substitute yogurt, which is equally delicious in this dressing. Believe me, as a former flesh eater, I guarantee this sauced-up falafel patty has more zest, flavor, and flare than Sean's retaliatory Tuesday Night (chicken and pig) Burger.

Sean

Tuesday Night Burger with Ginger-Lime Aioli

Burger Patties

1 teaspoon sesame oil
1 large onion, finely diced
2 cloves garlic, minced
1 tablespoon dried mint
¼ teaspoon red pepper flakes
1 teaspoon ground cinnamon
1 teaspoon ground cumin
½ pound ground lean chicken

½ pound ground pork
3 tablespoons chopped fresh cilantro
2 tablespoons Worcestershire sauce
Kosher salt and freshly ground black pepper to taste
8 strips bacon
1 tablespoon molasses
4 toasted black sesame seed buns

Burger Fixin's

2 tomatoes, sliced thick
4 fresh basil leaves, torn in half
1 English cucumber, sliced thin

1 red onion, sliced thin
1 cup shredded iceberg lettuce

For the burger patties, heat the oil and sauté the onion for 5 minutes. Add the garlic, mint, pepper flakes, cinnamon, and cumin, and sauté for 1 minute longer. Set aside to cool.

In a bowl, mix together the sautéed onion mixture, ground chicken, ground pork, cilantro, Worcestershire sauce, salt, and pepper. Shape into 4 equal patties about ½-inch thick and season each with a pinch more salt.

In a nonstick skillet, cook the patties, along with the bacon, for about 5 minutes on each side or until the center reads 165 degrees on a digital thermometer. Brush the burgers with the molasses and set aside for 5 minutes to rest.

Serve on toasted buns with the bacon, burger fixin's, and the aioli. Sit down with "Fresh Air" on NPR and enjoy.

Aioli

½ cup mayonnaise
¼ cup lime juice

1 tablespoon minced fresh ginger
¼ teaspoon paprika

Combine all ingredients in a food processor and blend thoroughly.

IF IT'S SUNDAY, Labor Day, or Game Day, grill up a beef patty. Saturday night makes it alright, but for a Tuesday night you need something that will rouse the mind, body, and spirit. This burger will get you over the hump and keep you going until the next day off. It also pairs nicely with a glass of Pino Grigio, rather than the gallons of water you are going to have to chug trying to choke down Maggie's ground sesame paste on a bun.

Southwest Black Bean Casserole

2 cups black beans, cooked or canned

2 cups diced heirloom tomatoes

1 organic green bell pepper, cored and chopped

2 cups shredded cheddar cheese

1 cup grated Parmesan cheese

1 yellow onion, minced

6 garlic cloves, minced or pressed

1 small jalapeño pepper, minced (remove seeds for milder taste)

1 cup chopped fresh cilantro

1 tablespoon ground cumin

1 tablespoon ground oregano

1 tablespoon ground coriander

1 teaspoon sea salt

1 teaspoon black pepper

Juice and zest of 1 organic lime

6 corn tortillas

Preheat the oven to 350 degrees. In a large mixing bowl, thoroughly mix all ingredients except the corn tortillas. Layer two corn tortillas in a well-oiled baking pan. Cover with a third of the bean mixture. Repeat layers to the top of the pan. Cover with foil and bake 1 hour.

. . . .

I AM NOT SURE HOW OR WHY this particular recipe stumped Sean, but it took him almost a year to give me a match to this. Maybe because it's so complete that it doesn't need any meat. This dish is a customer favorite at my café. It always sells out during our lunch rush. Each Christmas I make a pan of it for a customer who feeds it to her vegetarian son and daughter-in-law while they are home visiting. The best part of this dish, aside from its taste, is its ease. I should have called this one Toss and Bake (or Taos and Bake) because it takes hardly any time to prepare. It is all tossed together in one bowl with no sautéing, steaming, or blanching. All the meat eaters I know love a good Tex-Mex dish. This dish will integrate the table of cross eaters, and it can easily be converted to a vegan variation by simply omitting the cheese. All the amazing southwestern flavors are there with or without the dairy.

Sean

Nebraska White Beans and Rice

6 cups chicken stock

6 cups water

6 cloves garlic, cut into fourths

1 large yellow onion, diced

1 cup chopped celery

One 3-inch ham hock

1 teaspoon dried thyme

1 teaspoon dry mustard

1 tablespoon ground cumin

1 teaspoon ground sage

1 bay leaf

4 cups white rice

2 pounds garlic sausage links (preferably from Wahoo Locker in Wahoo, Nebraska), cut on the diagonal into ½-inch slices

½ cup James Arthur Heartland white wine

4 cups canned Great Northern beans, rinsed and drained

3 cups canned pinto beans, rinsed and drained

3 tablespoons horseradish

Kosher salt and freshly ground black pepper to taste

In a large stockpot, combine the chicken stock, water, garlic, onion, celery, ham hock, thyme, mustard, cumin, sage, and the bay leaf. Bring to a rolling boil over high heat and add the rice, sausage, and white wine. Stir to loosen anything sticking to the bottom. Reduce the heat to low and simmer for 4 minutes. Stir in the beans, remove the pot completely from the heat, and cover for 20 minutes. Stir one more time, adding the horseradish, salt, and pepper. Dish and devour.

• •

DID YOU KNOW NEBRASKA is the number-one producer of Great Northern beans in the United States? Yup. Number-three producer of pinto beans. True, we love our football, eat a lot of corn, and give directions in terms of time instead of distance but we are a culinary Mecca. People may not know where the state of Nebraska is per se (we are the one in the middle) but they love our food. Those are Omaha Steaks that Tokyo is calling for, and I guarantee that the sausages you get from the Wahoo Locker will rival the best you've ever had. When making this dish, and others as well, I suggest you get your spices from Brownville Mills (Nebraska's oldest health food store), buy your wine from James Arthur Vineyards, and start living the good life.

Wahoo Locker
157 West 5th Street
Wahoo NE 68066

Brownville Mills
P.O. Box 145
Brownville NE 68321

James Arthur Vineyards
2001 West Raymond Road
Raymond NE 68428

Eggplant Boat on the Mediterranean

3 organic eggplants
6 tablespoons olive oil
1 tablespoon sea salt
1 cup minced onion
3 tablespoons minced garlic
1 tablespoon fennel seed
2 cups chickpeas, cooked or canned
⅓ cup sherry

2 tablespoons balsamic vinegar
4 cups chopped heirloom tomatoes
1 green, red, or yellow bell pepper, minced
1 carrot, finely chopped
1 tablespoon dried oregano
1 cup minced fresh basil leaves
Zest of 1 organic lemon
1 cup pitted, halved kalamata olives

Brush a cookie sheet with 3 tablespoons of the olive oil. Cut each eggplant in half lengthwise. Make 3 lengthwise slits in the flesh, sprinkle with sea salt, and set aside for 10 minutes. When the eggplant begins to "sweat," rinse the salted halves and place cut side down on the sheet. Bake at 400 degrees for 10 to 15 minutes.

Sauté the onion, garlic, and fennel seed in the remaining 3 tablespoons of olive oil. When the onions are soft, add the chickpeas and allow the

flavors to marry. Add the sherry, balsamic vinegar, and tomatoes. Simmer 5 minutes. Add the green pepper, carrot, and oregano. Cook until most of the liquid is absorbed and the veggies are tender. Remove from the heat. Stir in the fresh basil, lemon zest, and kalamata olives.

Fill slits in the eggplant with the filling. Place the filled eggplant in a 9 × 13 baking pan. Cover with foil and return to the oven for 10 minutes.

• •

ONE OF MY FAVORITE THINGS about this dish is that the eggplant serves as an edible vessel. Some people don't eat the skin of the eggplant but I think it's the best part! I noted "organic" for the eggplant so that if you do eat the skin, you won't be consuming pesticide residue. There are some interesting colors of eggplant that would present themselves well in this dish, such as the lime hue of the Green Goddess, the vibrant violet Neon, or the pure whites of Cloud Nine and Bianca. If you are lucky enough to find an heirloom variety such as the Italian Listanda de Gandia or Antigua, use them! The same is true for the bell pepper — the more colors there are, the more unique the final presentation appears. Even if the only eggplant variety available is the grocery standard, you will still have an interesting filling full of color and flavors reminiscent of summer in Greece. The meat eaters at the table will be looking up from Sean's seafood-stuffed vegetable with curiosity, yearning for more insight into the eggplant world. Sean's seafood could never be as colorfully diverse. Ah, vegetarian options are endless . . .

Sean

Love Boat del Mar

3 eggplants

6 tablespoons olive oil

½ teaspoon ground cumin

½ teaspoon turmeric

1 teaspoon dried basil

½ cup diced yellow onion

¼ cup minced garlic

4 ounces 21/25 shrimp, peeled and deveined

½ cup lobster stock (fish broth can be substituted)

¼ cup lemon juice

1 tablespoon freshly ground fennel seed

1 medium green bell pepper, diced

1 tablespoon lemon zest

1 tablespoon dried oregano

¼ cup sherry

6 ounces bay scallops

6 ounces calamari tubes and tentacles, spine removed from tubes and cut into rings

4 cups finely diced Roma tomatoes

1 cup kalamata olives, pitted and halved

1½ tablespoons fresh basil leaves, chiffonade

2 tablespoons salted sweet cream butter

Kosher salt and pepper to taste

⅓ cup (3 ounces) crumbled feta cheese

¼ cup ouzo (Pernod can be substituted)

Preheat the oven to 375 degrees. Cut each eggplant in half lengthwise. Make 3 lengthwise slits in the flesh, then make 4 crosswise slits, creating a lattice look. Carefully, with a spoon or flexible knife, cut out the flesh, starting in the center and working your way toward the skin. Make sure that you don't cut through the skin; try to leave ⅛ inch of flesh still attached. Salt the eggplant shells and set aside for later.

In a bowl toss the removed eggplant flesh with 2 tablespoons of the olive oil, the cumin, turmeric, basil, and a pinch of salt. Transfer this mixture to a baking sheet and put it in the oven for 10 minutes or until it has a crisp golden-brown surface.

Heat 1 tablespoon of the olive oil in a large skillet or sauté pan over a high flame. Add the onions and cook until translucent. Add the garlic and shrimp and cook for 1 minute more. Stir in the lobster stock, lemon juice, fennel seed, green peppers, lemon zest, and oregano. Cook uncovered for 3 minutes, stirring constantly. Remove the pan from the heat and carefully add the sherry. Return the pan to the burner and add the scallops and calamari. Reduce the liquid by half, then remove from the heat. Toss in the tomatoes, olives, fresh basil, roasted eggplant flesh, butter, salt, and pepper. Combine thoroughly.

Rinse the salted eggplant boats and carefully, with a spoon, fill each cavity with the sautéed mixture. When filled, place them in a baking dish. Top the boats with feta cheese and drizzle with the ouzo. Bake uncovered for 6 minutes or until the top is *dore* (a beautiful golden brown).

THE LO-O-OVE BOAT soon will be converting vegetarians. A vegetarian's options might be endless, but ah, carnivore options are boundless. Why? Because we don't limit ourselves. As you herbivores look across the table from your "interesting fillings" and yearn for the bounty of the sea, have a taste. It's okay. We'll look the other way.

Garlic and Herb Roasted Summer Vegetables with Fresh Mozzarella

2 cups each: red onion, zucchini, yellow summer
    squash, red bell pepper, new potatoes, baby
    turnips, whole cherry tomatoes
¼ cup olive oil
6 tablespoons minced or pressed garlic
1 teaspoon sea salt
Freshly ground black pepper to taste

½ teaspoon dried oregano
½ teaspoon dried thyme
½ teaspoon dried basil
½ teaspoon crushed rosemary
1 pound thinly sliced fresh mozzarella cheese
Minced fresh parsley to garnish

Use a variety of vegetables that are in season at your local farmers' market. Cut vegetables in various shapes for an interesting visual presentation. Keep in mind that certain vegetables may take longer to roast, so cut their sizes accordingly. Some other vegetables to consider are yellow and green bell peppers, fennel, eggplant, mushrooms, carrots, asparagus, baby beets, or radishes.

Preheat the oven to 400 degrees. Toss the veggies with the olive oil, garlic, salt, pepper, oregano, basil, and rosemary. Spread on a baking sheet and roast uncovered 20 to 25 minutes. Top with fresh mozzarella slices and broil 2 to 3 minutes until cheese is golden brown. Garnish with parsley.

. . . .

EACH VEGETABLE BRINGS FORTH a burst of individual flavor that teases and tempts the palate bite after colorful bite. Whatever vegetables you decide to put into the mix, don't forget to use fresh tomatoes; they are necessary to complement the cheese and herbs. Use heirloom tomato varieties such as Yellow Pear, Black Pear, or Tommy Toes. A high-quality olive oil is also a good investment. The better the olive oil, the better the flavor. Look for a regionally produced cold-pressed olive oil. This dish has the versatility to change with every season. There's always a fresh veggie to be roasted any time of year. But there's not always that juicy burst of a seasonal tomato, which is why this recipe falls in summer's section.

Sean

Garlic and Herb Roasted Chicken with Vegetables

One 4- to 5-pound free-range chicken
1 medium yellow onion, chopped
4 cloves garlic, chopped
1 celery stalk, chopped
1 bay leaf
1 tablespoon dried Mexican oregano
1 tablespoon dried sage
1 lemon, sliced
1½ tablespoons olive oil
2 teaspoons kosher salt

Freshly ground black pepper to taste
1 large fennel bulb, cut into eighths
3 red potatoes, cut into eighths
6 brussels sprouts, cleaned and halved
2 large carrots, chopped
1 green bell pepper, chopped
1 teaspoon dried basil
1 teaspoon chopped fresh thyme
½ teaspoon chopped fresh mint

Preheat the oven to 350 degrees. After removing innards from the chicken, rinse it and pat it dry. In a bowl combine the onion, garlic, celery, bay leaf, oregano, sage, and half the lemon slices. Stuff this mixture into the cavity of the chicken. Rub the outside of the chicken with 1 tablespoon of the olive oil, 1 teaspoon of the salt, and pepper to taste. Let it sit on a baking rack and come to room temperature.

In a bowl combine the fennel, potatoes, brussels sprouts, carrots, bell pepper, basil, thyme, mint, and the remaining olive oil and salt; toss thoroughly. Spread the vegetables in a roasting pan and place the chicken on top of the vegetables, breast side down. Cover the chicken with the remaining lemon slices.

Roast for 1 hour or until the internal temperature of the chicken reaches 160 degrees. Let rest for 15 minutes before plating. Serve on a platter with the cooked vegetables.

• •

THE WONDROUS THING ABOUT CHICKEN is its adaptability. Chicken has a tranquil tenacity that enables it to harmonize with and enhance any flavor you pair it with. It is this ability that allows the chicken to transcend all seasons and give the chef an opportunity to use those delicious vegetables and their "burst of individual flavor."

Maggie

Spicy Hummus Stuffed Pita

4 whole-wheat pita pockets
1 cucumber, sliced
1 red onion, minced or thinly sliced
2 carrots, grated

2 heirloom tomatoes, chopped
2 ounces alfalfa sprouts
¼ cup toasted sesame seeds

Hummus

2 cups garbanzo beans, cooked or canned
½ cup chopped yellow onion
8 garlic cloves, chopped
½ cup lemon juice
½ cup olive oil (water can be substituted for lower-fat version)

1 tablespoon ground cumin
1 teaspoon sea salt
½ teaspoon cayenne pepper
½ teaspoon black pepper
⅓ cup tahini

For the hummus, place all ingredients except the tahini in a food processor. Blend until smooth. Add the tahini and continue to process until smooth and creamy.

Fill the pita pockets with hummus and add veggies as desired. Top with toasted sesame seeds. (To toast sesame seeds, place seeds in a dry skillet over medium heat until they begin to turn golden. Be careful not to overbrown or they will become bitter.)

· ·

THIS IS NOT YOUR TRADITIONAL Middle Eastern hummus. The pungent cumin and spicy cayenne give it a nice, unexpected twist. This is served at my café as a low-fat dish because water is substituted for the more commonly used olive oil. If you like a bright citrus flavor, use lemon juice for all the liquid in place of the oil. However, if you have a really good-quality olive oil, use it for its flavor. You could serve this dish up buffet-style. Arrange all the veggies in various dishes so the diners can choose to add as much or as little of their favorite toppings.

Sean

Honeydew Prawns with Chickpea Gazpacho Served in a Chilled Melon Bowl

Gazpacho

1 cup canned chickpeas, rinsed and drained
¼ cup breadcrumbs
½ cup chopped red onions
¼ cup chopped scallions
1 cup chopped celery
1 cup yellow bell pepper, seeded and chopped
1 cup green bell pepper, seeded and chopped
1 cup chopped cucumber, chopped

1 cup plum tomatoes, chopped
2 garlic cloves, crushed
¼ teaspoon cayenne pepper
¼ cup tomato paste
2 tablespoons rice wine vinegar
Juice and zest of 2 limes
1 cup water
1½ cups tomato juice

Combine all ingredients in a bowl and let sit in the refrigerator for 2 hours. In a food processor or blender, purée mixture until smooth. When you are ready to serve, pour the gazpacho into the melon bowl. Garnish with the prawns prepared from the recipe below. Serve cold.

Melon Bowl

2 medium honeydew melons

Juice of 1 lime

Trim ½ inch from each end of both honeydew melons. Halve the melons down the center; scoop out the seeds and discard. Scoop out and reserve the melon flesh, leaving the white areas still attached to the rind. Shower the bowls with lime juice and freeze until service.

Prawns

½ pound tail meat of freshwater prawns, bought fresh and chopped
Reserved scooped fruit from honeydew bowls

1 cup water
1 teaspoon Midori liqueur

In a food processor or blender, combine the melon, water, and liqueur. Purée until smooth. In a saucepot bring the purée to a simmer. Add the prawns and simmer for 5 minutes. Using a slotted spoon, remove the prawns and chill them. Discard the poaching liquid.

• •

THIS DISH IS AS REFRESHING as a walk through dew-glistened fields of green grass with trees budding on a spry April morn. Enjoy this dish when you need a sweet treat to beat the heat of July. Bask in its refreshment and relish its simplistic harmony. Other shellfish such as shrimp or any white fish can be substituted for the prawns. And vegetarians can remove the fish if they must, though they will miss the bliss. But what's this? A seasonal meat dish. My, oh my. Dear, dear.

   A word of warning about the fresh garlic content in Maggie's recipe. Eating her pita will leave you with burpy garlic breath for weeks afterward. So enjoy it, and chew some parsley as you sit dateless. Let the fact that you have just reduced your cholesterol by 200 points grant you solace.

Fall

Spinach and Squash Chickpeas in Creamy Coconut Sauce

3 tablespoons olive oil
2 cups minced yellow onion
10 garlic cloves, minced or pressed
1 tablespoon cumin seed
2 teaspoons sea salt
1 yellow crookneck squash or zucchini, peeled
    and cut into 1-inch cubes
1 tablespoon freshly grated ginger
½ teaspoon crushed red pepper flakes

One 14-ounce can coconut milk
2 cups chickpeas, cooked or canned
1 teaspoon ground coriander
1 teaspoon turmeric
½ teaspoon cayenne pepper
½ teaspoon ground cinnamon
Juice of 1 lime
2 pounds fresh spinach leaves
8 cups cooked basmati rice

Heat the olive oil in a sauté pan and add the onions, garlic, cumin seed, and salt. Cook until the onions are translucent, then add the squash, ginger, and red pepper flakes. Continue to cook on medium heat for another 10 minutes, stirring often. Add the coconut milk, chickpeas, coriander, turmeric, cayenne, and cinnamon. Cover and simmer until the squash is tender. Remove from the heat and stir in the lime juice and spinach leaves. Serve with basmati rice.

CURRIES ARE MY FAVORITE DISHES TO PREPARE. From turmeric to tandoori, the colors and flavors are so vibrant. Many of the spices used in curries have medicinal benefits and are often used in ayurvedic treatments. Turmeric has anti-inflammatory properties and cayenne improves circulation. Ginger reduces nausea and soothes upset stomachs. Cinnamon helps to regulate blood-sugar levels. This curry is made as a summer recipe but can easily be transformed into a winter dish by modifying the squash variety. Toward the end of the year when the chill is creeping into the air, use a heartier squash like butternut or acorn in place of the yellow crookneck or zucchini. The coconut base is neutral and goes either way according to season. While it's refreshing, light, and sweet in the summer, it can be warm, creamy, and satisfying in the winter. It's too bad that Sean's meat could never be so seasonally versatile. There are vegetables for every time of the year. Our bodies recognize and adapt to the temperature outside just as the ground knows when to sprout. The body craves different foods at different times of the year. The healthy vegetarian diet can adapt to those desires in the ways meat cannot. Sorry, Sean, back to the butcher's block.

Sean

Spinach and Squash Stuffed Capon Poached in Coconut Milk

4 boneless capon breasts, pounded very flat

1 teaspoon olive oil

1 shallot, minced

2 garlic cloves, minced

1 tablespoon pressed fresh ginger

1 small butternut squash, peeled and diced

¼ cup rice wine vinegar

1 tablespoon honey

Juice and zest of 1 lime

½ teaspoon crushed red pepper flakes

½ pound fresh baby spinach

4 sections of caul fat (To loosen the layers and prevent tearing, soak the caul fat in warm salted water before using.)

8 fresh sage leaves

One 14-ounce can coconut milk

1½ cups chicken stock or chicken broth

½ teaspoon ground cumin

1 teaspoon turmeric

1 bay leaf

Kosher salt and ground white pepper to taste

Heat the olive oil in a large sauté pan over medium to high heat. Add the shallots and cook for 1 minute. Add the garlic and ginger and sauté 1 minute longer. Toss in the squash and deglaze the pan with the rice wine vinegar. Stir in the honey, lime juice, red pepper flakes, and salt. Continue cooking until the liquid is almost completely evaporated. Transfer to a bowl and mix in the spinach and lime zest. Let cool to a manageable temperature.

Spread out a section of caul fat, place two fresh sage leaves in the middle, and lay a rooster breast flat on top. Season with the salt and pepper. Spoon ¼ cup of the squash mixture near the middle of the edge facing you. Roll up only the capon breast, tightly, and overlap with the other edge of the breast. Bring in the sides and gently but tightly wrap the entire stuffed capon breast with the caul fat. Repeat with each remaining capon breast.

In a high-sided skillet bring half of the coconut milk and 1 cup of the chicken stock to a boil. Reduce to a simmer and add the rolled capon breasts. Cover and simmer for 30 minutes or until the internal temperature of the capon breast reaches 160 degrees.

In a saucepot combine the rest of the coconut milk, chicken stock, cumin, turmeric, bay leaf, salt, and pepper and bring to a slow boil. Reduce by two-thirds. Spoon ¼ cup of the sauce on each plate and gently place the capon breast in the center of the sauce. Drizzle a little additional sauce over the top and enjoy.

• •

THE CAPON IS A YOUNG, FATTENED ROOSTER. Its juicy flavor is a bit more robust than that of a chicken. Chicken, pork tenderloin, or veal could also be used here if the thought of a rooster doesn't make you crow. The key is to wrap the breast tightly and make sure that the flesh from one side overlaps flesh of the other side before you wrap it tightly, again, in caul fat. When you reduce the boiling poaching liquid to a simmer, you want to see just a couple of bubbles trickling up—a lazy simmer that gently rocks the stuffed capon into a gastronomic heaven.

Caul fat is the fatty membrane that lines the abdominal cavity of a sheep or pig. Once you get past that fact, you will find it to be a valuable tool in method and presentation. Generally caul fat is used to wrap pâté or forcemeat, but I like to apply it to everyday meals, jazzing things up a bit. As it cooks, the fatty membrane melts away and what you have left is the beautiful lacey net that, in this case, helps hold the rolled breast together and all the deliciousness inside. Both capons and caul fat can be acquired from your local butcher.

Now, I'm sure Maggie has plenty to say about using the lining of a pig's stomach. But for me it speaks to the both the philosophy of life and the pursuit of "total utilization," which is a way of appreciating life by not letting anything be wasted. Using everything in a satisfying, artful way endows gratitude for what has been provided.

Deglazing is done by adding a small amount of liquid to the pan after or during sautéing. It helps to loosen the tasty bits of food and flavor that stick to the pan, allowing every hint of essence to make it to the plate.

I have to laugh, and cry a little, when I hear vegetarians naively rattle on about how meat can't be seasonal. This portion of the population shamefully misses out on the first catch of halibut season, which fills my taste buds with as much anticipation as that first harvest of asparagus. I'm sorry, Maggie, that you've chosen to miss out on sheer joy of oyster soup at Christmas, saucy summer briskets, a hot dog on opening day, a spring lamb, pheasant in the fall, the flavor of ribeye steaks mixing with aroma of freshly cut grass on a warm August evening.

To quote you: "The body craves different foods at different times of the year." And there is a time every year that I know for certain makes you question your own convictions, Maggie, my dear: turkey on Thanksgiving.

One of the benefits of eating a complete diet is being able to enjoy the seasons by eating the foods that are traditionally part of them. And one of the benefits of not restricting my "complete" diet is being able to enjoy the "seasonal" meat right next to those "seasonal" veggies you are always totin' around.

Seasonal Lasagna

10 uncooked lasagna noodles

Balsamic Marinated Tomatoes

2 cups diced heirloom tomatoes
2 tablespoons balsamic vinegar
2 tablespoons olive oil

2 tablespoons minced fresh basil
1 tablespoons minced or pressed garlic
Sea salt and black pepper to taste

Combine all ingredients and set aside to marinate for 1 hour at room temperature.

Cottage Cheese Mixture

2 pounds cottage cheese
1 cup minced red onion
1 cup chopped fresh parsley
1¼ cups Parmesan cheese, plus ½ cup set aside for topping
3 tablespoons minced or pressed garlic

1 teaspoon black pepper
2 teaspoons dried oregano
2 teaspoons dried basil
2 teaspoons fennel seed
½ teaspoon red pepper flakes

Preheat the oven to 375 degrees. Combine all ingredients for the cottage cheese mixture in a large bowl, reserving ½ cup Parmesan cheese for the topping. In a 9 × 13 baking pan spread the bottom with half of the balsamic tomato mixture, then layer the noodles alternately with the cottage cheese mixture. Between the layers, add any combination of your choice of seasonal vegetables, such as asparagus, artichoke hearts, roasted red peppers, spinach, butternut squash, or mushrooms. For the top layer, use the remaining half of the balsamic tomato mixture and top with the Parmesan cheese. Bake, covered, for 1 hour.

• •

I LOVE LASAGNA! It's such a work of art. Everything from the produce to the process is a true artistic expression of the chef. This is the summer version utilizing fresh tomatoes, but anything goes for lasagna — there are no rules. Toss in some fresh peppers or zucchini if you want. Lasagna has the versatility to work in every season — light asparagus in spring lasagna, savory fresh tomato in summer lasagna, hearty squash in fall lasagna, and warm root vegetables in winter lasagna. There is probably a lasagna recipe for every day of the year, but that's another cookbook. Here's where Sean really misses out. The vegetable kingdom is far more vast than the breeds of edible animals. From its 4,230,642,791 variations, you could make a vegetarian lasagna every day for the rest of your life and never make the same one twice.

Sean

Lasagna the Right Way

½ cup pancetta, cubed
4 anchovy fillets, chopped
3 garlic cloves, minced
1 teaspoon olive oil
½ pound ground pork
¼ pound ground beef
2 teaspoons dried oregano
2 teaspoons dried basil
2 teaspoons freshly ground fennel seed
½ teaspoon red pepper flakes

¼ cup tomato paste
1 cup canned tomatoes
½ cup red wine
2 pounds cottage cheese
1 cup minced red onion
1 cup chopped fresh parsley
1¼ cups freshly grated Parmesan cheese
1 teaspoon freshly ground black pepper
1 pound uncooked lasagna noodles
1½ cups shredded mozzarella

In a saucepot over medium to high heat, sauté the pancetta, anchovies, and garlic in the olive oil until golden. Remove the garlic and reserve. To the same skillet add the ground pork, ground beef, oregano, basil, fennel seed, and red pepper flakes. Brown well. Add the tomato paste, tomatoes, and wine. Simmer over medium heat until the liquid is reduced by half.

In a bowl combine the cottage cheese, onion, parsley, Parmesan cheese, pepper, and the reserved garlic. Spray the sides and bottom of a 9 × 13 baking pan with cooking oil. Spoon a thin layer of the meat mixture on the bottom of the pan. Cover it with a layer of lasagna noodles, a layer of the cottage cheese mixture, and a layer of shredded mozzarella. Continue this process and end with a layer of meat sauce and top with mozzarella. Cover the pan with foil and refrigerate overnight.

Preheat the oven to 375 degrees. Bake, covered, for 45 minutes. Uncover and bake another 10 minutes. Serve hot and *provare gioia*!

• •

MAYBE IT'S JUST ME, and about a billion others, but I think lasagna needs some meat. Don't get me wrong — I have had some really fantastic vegetable lasagnas. I have even craved them and made some myself. I have also had exquisite seafood lasagnas, but a good old Sunday Night Lasagna, to me, needs meat — more specifically, ground pork. That flavor just permeates the whole dish and says "I love you" with each mouthwatering bite. I also believe that in order for your red sauce to have a good "base," it needs anchovies.

Maggie has to pull out her abacus again. I don't think she understands that I do not put limits on the food I eat. Therefore I do not "miss out" on anything and get to enjoy the every aspect of taste, not just the green leafy one. While I won't throw out some arbitrary, made-up number, I am sure you could live at least seven lifetimes and never eat the same lasagna with meat.

Quinoa Stuffed Peppers with Black Bean Mojo

4 large bell peppers (1 each: red, yellow, orange, green)

Cut the peppers in half lengthwise and remove the seeds. Place tightly together, cavity side up, in a large baking dish. Fill the dish ¼ inch deep with salted water. Set aside. Preheat the oven to 400 degrees.

Quinoa Stuffing

1 tablespoon peanut oil
1 tablespoon cumin seed
1 jalapeño pepper, seeded and minced
1 garlic clove, minced
4 scallions, chopped
10 to 12 sun-dried tomatoes, halved
4 cups water with 1 tablespoon sea salt added
2 cups uncooked quinoa
½ cup toasted pumpkin seeds
½ cup chopped fresh cilantro
Juice of 1 lime

Heat the peanut oil in a 3-quart sauté pan. Add the cumin seed and fry until the seeds begin to "pop." Add the jalapeño, garlic, scallions, and tomatoes and sauté until softened. Add the sea-salted water and bring to a boil. Add quinoa and return to a boil, then reduce to a simmer and cover. Cook 20 to 30 minutes or until all liquid is absorbed. Remove from the heat and stir in the pumpkin seeds, cilantro, and lime juice. Fill each pepper in the baking dish with the quinoa filling. Cover the baking dish with foil and bake for 15 to 20 minutes.

(To toast pumpkin seeds, place the seeds in a dry skillet until they begin to "pop" or place them on a baking sheet in a preheated 400-degree oven for 5 minutes.)

Black Bean Mojo

1 onion, chopped
6 garlic cloves, minced or pressed
2 cups black beans, cooked or canned
1 cup tomato sauce
1 teaspoon sea salt
2 teaspoons dried oregano
1 teaspoon ground cumin
1 teaspoon ground coriander

Sauté the onion and garlic until golden. Add black beans, tomato sauce, salt, oregano, cumin, and coriander. Cover and simmer for 10 minutes. Remove from the heat. Using an immersion blender or food processor, purée the bean mixture until it is smooth and creamy. Add water for desired consistency. Arrange the multicolored peppers on serving plates. Drizzle with Black Bean Mojo.

• •

DATING BACK TO THE ANCIENT INCAS, quinoa, pronounced "keen-wah," is known as the super grain. It contains all eight amino acids, making it a complete protein. Cortez was said to have fed it to his army for its reputed superpowers! It cooks up like rice but in half the time, expanding to four times its original size. I love its delicate flavor, texture, and unique shape. Quinoa is commonly available at health food stores. Why not get all your protein in one tasty grain instead of from chicken organs and pig byproducts? The answer seems simple to me, Sean. All the protein in this dish comes entirely from the plant kingdom, so vegans can indulge in the nutritious absence of dairy and eggs. Without the addition of cheese or sour cream, this is also a low-calorie recipe that won't weigh you down on a hot summer day. The spice in the stuffed peppers and mojo sauce can be complimented with refreshing lime margaritas! Party on the patio!

Sean

Dirty Rice Stuffed Peppers with Black Bean Mojo

Dirty Rice Stuffed Peppers

2 large red bell peppers
2 large yellow bell peppers
4 tablespoons butter or bacon drippings
6 ounces ground chicken gizzards
6 ounces ground chicken livers
4 ounces lean ground pork or beef
¾ cup diced yellow onion
½ cup chopped celery
½ cup diced green bell pepper
3 cups chicken stock or broth

1 garlic clove, minced
1 bay leaf
¼ teaspoon ground white pepper
½ teaspoon freshly ground black pepper
½ teaspoon cayenne pepper
½ teaspoon ground cumin
½ teaspoon dried oregano
1 tablespoon kosher salt
1½ cups rice
½ cup finely shredded scallions

Black Bean Mojo

1 medium yellow onion, diced
6 garlic cloves, chopped
Reserved seeds and flesh of the bell peppers
2 cups canned black beans, drained and rinsed
1 cup tomato sauce

2 teaspoon dried oregano
1 teaspoon ground cumin
1 teaspoon ground coriander
1 teaspoon salt

Remove the tops of the red and yellow bell peppers and scoop out the seeds and white flesh. Reserve the flesh and seeds for the black bean mojo. Set the peppers aside.

For the dirty rice, heat a heavy-duty saucepan or cast-iron skillet over a medium flame. Melt 3 tablespoons of the butter or bacon drippings and add the ground gizzards and the ground pork or beef. Brown the meat thoroughly, stirring constantly, about 5 minutes. Add the onion, celery, and green pepper and cook for about 2 minutes. Add ½ cup of the chicken stock and cook for 4 to 5 minutes, scraping the bottom and sides of the pan with a metal spoon. Add the ground chicken livers and the remaining 2½ cups of chicken stock, along with the garlic, bay leaf, white pepper, black pepper, cayenne, cumin, oregano, and salt, and bring to a boil. Let simmer for 2 minutes.

Stir in the rice and cover the saucepan. Turn the heat to very low and cook for 17 minutes. Turn the oven to broil. Uncover the pot of rice and stir in the shredded scallions. Fill the hollow red and yellow bell peppers with the dirty rice and replace the pepper tops. Drizzle the stuffed peppers with the remaining tablespoon of margarine or drippings and set aside.

For the black bean mojo, sauté the onion, garlic, and the reserved pepper seeds and flesh until golden brown. Add the black beans, tomato sauce, oregano, cumin, coriander, and salt. Cover and simmer for 10 minutes. Remove from the heat. Using an immersion blender or food processor, purée until smooth and creamy.

Place the stuffed peppers in a baking dish and broil for 4 minutes in the lower center of the oven. Remove the pan and drizzle the stuffed peppers with the black bean mojo. Serve hot and enjoy.

⟨⟨ THIS CAJUN DISH MAY NOT LOOK SO GREAT, because the meat gives the rice the appearance of being dirty, but the payoff is a betrothal of delicious flavors that yield a rich and yummy love. I bow to the culinary talent of the chef, clearly a firm believer in the total utilization philosophy, who through sheer genius or mere accident gave the world this truly enchanting dish.

You can replace the livers and gizzards with sausage, though I strenuously recommend you don't. And I really recommend that you use bacon fat instead of butter. It may make your physician shake her head, but bring her some and she'll understand.

I think you will find the combination of mojo and dirty rice more satisfying than mojo and Maggie's gritty, bland "super grain."

Black Bean and Sweet Potato Cakes with Jalapeño-Chive Sour Cream

Jalapeño-Chive Sour Cream

1 cup sour cream
½ cup fresh minced chives
1 tablespoon lemon juice

2 to 3 jalapeños, minced (remove seeds for milder taste)
Sea salt and pepper to taste

Mix all ingredients in a small bowl until well blended. Set aside to infuse the flavors.

Cakes

2 pounds sweet potatoes, cooked and mashed
2 cups black beans, cooked or canned
1 to 2 tablespoons chili oil
1½ cups cheddar cheese
¼ cup minced scallions or chives
1 tablespoon cornmeal

2 tablespoons ground flax seed
2 teaspoons dried oregano
1 tablespoon toasted cumin seed
1 teaspoon dried tarragon
2 teaspoons sea salt
2 teaspoons black pepper

Preheat the oven to 400 degrees (if baking). Bake or boil the sweet potatoes with the skins on until tender. Cool, remove the skins, and mash the sweet potatoes with a fork. In a food processor, blend the chili oil, cheese, scallions, cornmeal, flax seed, oregano, cumin seed, tarragon, salt, and pepper. Transfer to a mixing bowl. Stir in the black beans and mashed sweet potatoes. Form the mixture into patties and fry in a large skillet until golden and encrusted. Serve warm with Jalapeño-Chive Sour Cream.

(To toast cumin seed, place in a dry skillet and heat until fragrant, stirring constantly.)

. . . .

THIS RECIPE MAKES APPROXIMATELY 12 to 14 cakes. As a main dish, serve 3 or 4 cakes for each person. These can also be made in miniature for an appetizer. They always go over really well at potlucks. The use of flax seed serves two purposes in this recipe. One, it substitutes for egg, which would otherwise be used as the binding agent. Two, it parallels the health benefits of Sean's salmon. Flax seed is the richest plant source of omega-3 fatty acids. Not only does it not contain cholesterol but it actually helps to reduce it. Salmon ain't all that. For a lower-fat version of this dish, bake the cakes on a cookie sheet rather than frying them. Bake at 400 degrees for 15 to 20 minutes, flipping the cakes over halfway through.

Sean

Salmon Cakes with Jalapeño-Mint Mayo

Salmon Cakes

1 pound fresh wild salmon, skin removed and coarsely chopped
4 tablespoons mayonnaise
2 teaspoons Dijon mustard
2 tablespoons capers, drained and rinsed
3 tablespoons minced Vidalia onion
1 tablespoon thinly sliced scallion

Salt and pepper to taste
¾ cup panko or other breadcrumbs
1 teaspoon olive oil
8 ounces Swiss chard
¼ cup red onion, sliced paper thin
4 fresh dill fronds

In a bowl combine the salmon, mayonnaise, Dijon mustard, capers, onion, scallion, salt, and pepper. Using a rubber spatula, mix until all ingredients are well incorporated. Using your hands, turn the salmon mixture into stout patties roughly 1 inch in diameter and 1¾ inch in height. Dredge the patties in the breadcrumbs and refrigerate for 1 hour.

Preheat the oven to 350 degrees. Heat the olive oil in a skillet over medium to high heat. When the oil comes up to temperature (it will crackle with a single drop of water), add the salmon cakes and sear. When the bottom of the cake resembles the color of the prairie at dusk in August (a slight golden brown) flip and sear the other side. When both sides have been seared, transfer the cakes to a baking sheet and bake for 7 minutes.

Divide the Swiss chard between four plates, top the greens with three hot cakes, drizzle with jalapeño-mint mayo, and garnish with thinly sliced red onions and fresh dill. Serve warm and lap it up.

Jalapeño-Mint Mayo

1 jalapeño pepper, stemmed and seeded
1 cup mayonnaise

½ cup cilantro
1 tablespoon freshly squeezed lemon juice

Combine all ingredients in a food processor and blend until smooth.

· ·

I'M FAIRLY CERTAIN, and I think Maggie will agree, that I can tempt any vegetarian to come back home to the carnivore side of the table with these beauties. Even if you are on the side of the "fully fed" but you think salmon just isn't your kettle of fish, you should give these cakes a try. The salmon flavor that can throw some people off is subdued with the commingling of the mustard and mayo. Then new flavors are brought to life with the jalapeño-mint dressing, and before you lose yourself in the clouds of ecstasy you look down and see that your plate is clean.

For the vegetarian who's feeling guilty desires, I leave you with some quasi-Plato to learn and live by: "A dish is not desirable because it is tasted but tasted because it is desirable."

White Eggplant Parmesan

White Sauce

1 cup butter
½ cup flour
1 tablespoon sea salt
1 teaspoon white pepper

1 teaspoon dried oregano
1 teaspoon crushed rosemary
4 cups milk

Eggplant Parmesan

6 white eggplants, unpeeled
12 Roma tomatoes
6 cups coarsely shredded Parmesan cheese

2 cups fresh basil leaves
1 cup breadcrumbs

Preheat the oven to 350 degrees. For the White Sauce, melt the butter in a saucepan. Sprinkle the flour into the melted butter little by little, continuously whisking to prevent lumps. When all the flour has been added, add sea salt, white pepper, oregano, and rosemary. Add milk one cup at a time, whisking constantly, until the sauce is smooth and creamy. When the sauce thickens, turn the heat to very low and keep the sauce warm.

Cut the eggplant and the tomatoes into ½-inch slices. In a large baking dish, layer half the eggplant, tomatoes, Parmesan cheese, basil leaves, and White Sauce. Repeat these layers using the remaining half of the ingredients and top with the breadcrumbs. Cover and bake 30 to 35 minutes. Uncover and bake 5 minutes to brown the top.

· ·

THIS IS NOT YOUR AVERAGE EGGPLANT PARMESAN. The white sauce breaks away from the traditional marinara base, as does the color of the eggplant itself. If you can't find the white variety of eggplant, use whatever is available to you. Any eggplant variety is more humane than a baby cow that lived its stunted life without fresh air or sunshine. The eggplant's tender texture is a tasty, guilt-free alternative to the immobile flesh of veal. Sean should serve a side of conscience with his dish.

Sean

Veal Parmesan

4 veal cutlets
1 box panko or Italian breadcrumbs
2 tablespoons all-purpose flour
1 tablespoon dried basil
1 teaspoon dry mustard
1 teaspoon garlic powder

1 tablespoon ground fennel seed
¼ cup freshly grated Parmesan reggiano cheese
1 teaspoon kosher salt
Freshly ground black pepper to taste
6 tablespoons vegetable oil

Combine the panko, flour, basil, dry mustard, garlic powder, fennel seed, Parmesan cheese, salt, and pepper in a shallow pan and mix thoroughly. Dredge the veal cutlets in the mixture. In a frying pan heat the oil over a medium flame. Fry the veal cutlets until golden brown on both sides. Serve over the pasta of your choice topped with marinara sauce.

• • • • • • • • • • • • • • • • •

"

Veal is good. And I sleep just fine at night.

Winter

Wild Mushroom Seitan Stroganoff

2 tablespoons olive oil
1 cup coarsely chopped leeks
2 garlic cloves, chopped
½ pound sliced porcini mushrooms
½ pound sliced button mushrooms
½ pound sliced portobello mushrooms
1 teaspoon white pepper
2 bay leaves

1 teaspoon crushed rosemary
1 pound finely chopped seitan (wheat gluten
  meat substitute)
½ pint sour cream
¼ cup soy sauce
¼ cup sherry
8 ounces uncooked egg noodles
1 teaspoon truffle oil

Heat the olive oil and sauté the leeks and garlic for 5 minutes. Add the mushrooms, white pepper, bay leaves, and rosemary. Continue cooking until the mushrooms are soft. Stir in the seitan, sour cream, soy sauce, sherry, and noodles. Cover and cook until the noodles are tender, adding liquid if necessary. Remove from the heat and stir in the truffle oil.

. . . .

YOU COULD SUBSTITUTE OTHER MUSHROOMS, such as morels, criminis, oysters, or chanterelles, and really get some exciting flavors going on. Some of the wild mushrooms may only be available dried in the winter. Don't let this deter you from using these gems — simply reconstitute them with a little hot water and they're good to go. I have made this dish for some of the most "meat and potato" people I know and they swooned. This rich, creamy dish is quite robust with the mushrooms and the hearty seitan. Alone, the mushrooms make this a meaty dish, but it really "beefs" up when combined with the meatlike texture and protein of the seitan. Derived from wheat gluten, seitan is an excellent low-fat, cholesterol-free source of protein and iron. Its comfort-food qualities would win the heart of Sean's meat-and-potato eaters. I highly recommend the splurge on truffle oil. It is an essential ingredient to this dish.

Sean

Beef Stroganoff

1 cup all-purpose flour

1 teaspoon onion powder

1 teaspoon garlic powder

¼ teaspoon freshly ground nutmeg

Kosher salt and freshly ground black pepper to taste

1 8-ounce package Ha-Lush-Ka or other egg noodles

1 teaspoon butter

2 tablespoons olive oil

½ pound beef chuck roast, cubed

1 diced yellow onion

1 garlic clove, minced

2 cups beef stock or beef broth

1 cup sliced porcini mushrooms

1 cup sliced crimini mushrooms

1 cup morel mushrooms, stemmed and sliced

1 teaspoon chopped fresh thyme

1 teaspoon chopped fresh savory

2 tablespoons chopped fresh chives

1 tablespoon Dijon mustard

¼ cup cooking sherry

1 cup sour cream

In a bowl sift together the flour, onion powder, garlic powder, nutmeg, salt, and pepper. Cook the noodles according to the package instructions, drain and toss the noodles with the butter. In a large skillet heat the olive oil over medium to high heat. Dredge the beef cubes in the flour mixture and brown on all sides in the hot oil. Add the onion and garlic and reduce the heat to medium. Sauté until the onions are translucent. Deglaze the pan with several tablespoons of the beef stock, if nec-essary. Add the mushrooms, thyme, savory, chives, and Dijon mustard. Sauté for 1 minute longer. Move the pan away from the flame and stir in the sherry. Season with salt and pepper and return to the flame; be careful of flame-ups. Simmer until the sherry is reduced by half and add the remaining beef stock. Simmer until the liquid is again reduced by half. Incorporate the sour cream and serve hot over the buttered noodles. Savor the yumminess.

• •

OF COURSE THOSE "MEAT AND POTATO" EATERS SWOONED. Mushrooms are delicious! But I bet they ate meat the next day. The comfort of Beef Stroganoff doesn't come just from eating hot creamy noodles on a cool day but from gently marrying the subtle flavors of the beef, cream, and mushrooms. The wondrous flavor, aroma, and comfort of this marriage is what Maggie is trying to achieve with her substitution of seitan. But ultimately that combination of flavors is missed — and longed for.

Maggie

Bolshevik Beet-n-Blue Gratin

1 pound Yukon Gold potatoes
1 pound chioggia or red beets, with green tops
3 tablespoons olive oil
1 tablespoon vinegar
1 tablespoon Dijon mustard
½ teaspoon fennel seed
½ teaspoon caraway seed

1 teaspoon sea salt
1 teaspoon black pepper
1 cup crumbled blue cheese
1 cup cottage cheese
1½ cups toasted walnuts
½ cup chopped fresh parsley

Preheat the oven to 400 degrees. Cut the washed, unpeeled potatoes crosswise into 1-inch-thick slices. Set aside. Remove the green tops from the beets; wash and set aside the greens. Peel and cut the beets into 1-inch-thick slices. For marinade, whisk together the olive oil, vinegar, Dijon mustard, fennel seed, caraway seed, salt, and pepper.

Toss the sliced beets in the marinade until well coated. In a shallow baking dish, alternate layers of marinated beets, blue cheese, cottage cheese, beet greens, and potatoes. Finish the top layer with the remaining cheeses and the walnuts. Cover with foil and bake for 30 minutes. Garnish with fresh parsley.

. . . .

I CAN'T PRAISE BEETS ENOUGH. Opposites attract with the salty tang of the blue cheese and the sweet earthiness of the beets. Who says winter has to be void of fresh flavors? The Earth's heart*beet* is in its roots, alive and pulsing in the ground. Nothing says love on a cold, wintry Valentine's Day like the beet's crimson heart. There are, of course, other varieties of beets that can be put into the love pot. The heirloom chiogga or golden beets lack the red intensity but are more interesting for their own unique flavor and color. Any beet variety will go well in this dish. The boldness of the blue cheese with the softness of the beet is the perfect marriage of tastes.

Sean

Salmon and Tuna Carpaccio with Roasted Beets

2 chioggia beets, with green tops
4 golden baby beets
3 tablespoons olive oil
Kosher salt and freshly ground black pepper to
    taste
Eight 2-ounce slices sushi-grade tuna
Eight 2-ounce center-cut salmon fillets
½ teaspoon dry mustard

1 tablespoon minced shallot
2 fresh basil leaves, coarsely chopped
2 tablespoons cane vinegar
⅓ cup lavender oil
1 cup chopped mustard greens
½ cup chopped radicchio
1 cup (8 ounces) crumbled chèvre cheese
⅓ cup (3 ounces) toasted chopped pistachios

Preheat the oven to 375 degrees. Remove the green tops of the beets, leaving ½ inch on the beet. Wash and chop the greens and reserve them for later. Rub the beets with the olive oil, salt, and pepper and roast for 45 minutes or until a fork is easily inserted (fork tender). Allow the beets to cool; then carefully, with gloved hands, remove the skins. Slice thinly and refrigerate.

Stretch a sheet of plastic wrap on a flat cutting board or countertop. Sprinkle the plastic wrap with olive oil and place a slice of tuna or a salmon fillet in the middle. Place another piece of plastic wrap on top and ever so gently pound the slice flat using a mallet or sauté pan. Put the flattened fish in the refrigerator for plating. Repeat with the remaining slices of tuna and salmon fillets. In a large bowl combine the dry mustard, shallot, fresh basil, and cane vinegar. Slowly add 3 ounces of the lavender oil, whisking constantly. Toss into the dressing bowl the mustard greens, radicchio, and the reserved beet greens. Divide the greens between four plates. Beside the greens on the plate, alternate layers of salmon, golden beets, tuna, and red beets. Garnish the greens with the chèvre cheese and toasted pistachios and drizzle the remaining lavender oil over the layered fish (a very small amount per plate). Serve chilled and enjoy.

. . . .

LAVENDER HAS AN INTOXICATING BOUQUET that endures the earthy strength of the roasted beets. But lavender oil can be pricey and hard to find, so feel free to substitute vegetable or pistachio oil until you pick up some lavender buds and infuse some oil of your own.

I have to agree with Maggie's praise of beets. As a young boy, at the dinner table my hands and lips were stained a bright crimson as I gobbled them up. I have long been fascinated by these astounding orbs that have a flavor as dark and rich as their flesh.

To the people who say they don't like beets, Maggie and I will both tell you, "Bolshevik! You just haven't given them a chance!"

SERVES 4

Hungarian Tempeh Goulash

2 tablespoons olive oil

2 Yukon Gold or red potatoes, cubed

2 carrots, chopped

2 celery stalks, chopped

1 green bell pepper, cored and chopped

1 yellow onion, chopped

1 teaspoon salt

1 teaspoon caraway seed

1½ cups tomato sauce

½ cup vegetable broth

1 bay leaf

One 8-ounce package tempeh, crumbled

2 tablespoons Hungarian paprika

2 teaspoons sea salt

1 teaspoon black pepper

1 tablespoon olive oil

1 cup sour cream

Heat the olive oil in a sauté pan. Add the potatoes, carrots, celery, bell pepper, onion, salt, and caraway seed and sauté for 10 to 15 minutes or until the veggies begin to soften. Add the tomato sauce, vegetable broth, and bay leaf. Cover and simmer for 15 minutes.

Toss the tempeh with the paprika, salt, and pepper until evenly coated. Heat the olive oil in a sauté pan and cook the tempeh for 5 to 10 minutes until encrusted and browned. Add the tempeh to the simmering veggies. Continue simmering until the veggies are tender. Remove from the heat. Stir in the sour cream. Serve immediately with rye bread. Garnish with fresh dill and dollops of sour cream.

. . . .

THE ONLY SIMILARITIES SEAN AND I HAVE over goulash are that we both love it in the winter and neither of us stayed true to our grandmas. My grandma would have used plenty of ground cow meat and probably some pig fat. When my mom made it, she also used meat but added macaroni noodles and used a straight tomato base. I like the addition of sour cream. It definitely smoothes out the tomato sauce, and along with the spices, gives it that distinct eastern European flavor. The texture of the tempeh is similar to ground meat and adds more protein. I suggest Yukon or red potatoes, but any potatoes are good in this dish. Notice that Sean is catching my vegetable variety vibe and mimicking it in his comeback. I will agree with Sean that goulash is one of the great comfort foods. This is the lighter, simpler, and tastier vegetarian version. So you can take comfort in knowing that you will be eating healthy with enough nutrition to keep the body warm through a cold winter's night — no quilt required.

Sean

SERVES 4

G-Ma's Goulash

3 tablespoons vegetable oil
1 pound round steak, cubed
3 medium onions, chopped
½ teaspoon kosher salt
¼ teaspoon black pepper
½ teaspoon garlic salt
1 bay leaf
1 teaspoon Hungarian paprika

¼ teaspoon sugar
2¼ cups cold water
⅓ cup crushed tomatoes
2¼ cups water
9 Russian banana fingerling potatoes, rinsed
1 large carrot, chopped
1 tablespoon all-purpose flour
½ cup heavy whipping cream

Heat the vegetable oil in a large frying pan or Dutch oven. Add meat cubes and brown well, approximately 10 minutes. Stir in onions; cook until soft. Sprinkle with kosher salt, pepper, garlic salt, bay leaf, paprika, and sugar and blend thoroughly. Add 2 cups of the water and the crushed tomatoes. Add the potatoes and carrots; cover and simmer gently about 1½ hours.

In a bowl, whisk the flour with ¼ cup of cold water. Be sure to break up any lumps. Add to the meat about 7 minutes before the end of the cooking time. Stir constantly until the sauce is thickened and bubbling. Remove from the heat; stir in the whipping cream. Ladle the goulash into individual bowls and add a dollop of sour cream for good measure. Serve hot and subsist *megelégedett*.

GOULASH, TO ME, is one of the great comfort foods. It is perfect on the snowman days when your toes feel like annoying pebbles in your shoe. Or when the sun disappears before five o'clock, traffic on the drive home runs like a frozen crick, and all you want is a hearty meal that will warm your bones enough to make it to the ten o'clock news while you're lying in bed wrapped in a quilt that holds the spiced smell of generations long past.

To be fair, this isn't my grandma's recipe. She used to make her goulash with egg noodles instead of potatoes, but goulash still reminds me of chilly days in Central City, Nebraska, and the warmth that my grandma's house seemed to be brimming with. Though I prefer the noodles, the dish is traditionally prepared with potatoes. I use Russian banana fingerlings because, for me, they add an authentic flavor. But any kind of potatoes will do. For a crazy weird experience try using purple potatoes.

I don't see tempeh holding back the galling ice breezes whistling past the window, so you veg heads will probably need an extra quilt or two.

Seitan Satay over Golden Rice

Golden Rice

2 cups basmati rice
3½ cups water with 1 tablespoon sea salt added
2 cups chopped fresh cilantro

1 tablespoon ghee or butter
1 teaspoon turmeric

Rinse the basmati rice in a colander until the water runs clear. Transfer the rice to a stockpot. Add the salted water, cilantro, ghee, and turmeric. Bring to a boil. Reduce the heat to a simmer; cover and cook the rice for 30 minutes or until the water is absorbed and the rice is tender. Remove from the heat and fluff with a fork until cilantro and rice are well combined.

Peanut Sauce

1 cup creamy peanut butter
½ cup soy sauce
½ cup canned coconut milk
½ cup *toasted* sesame oil
¼ cup honey or brown sugar
¼ cup lemon juice
6 garlic cloves, minced or pressed
6 scallions, chopped

2 tablespoons chopped fresh basil
2 tablespoon chopped fresh cilantro
1 tablespoon grated fresh ginger
1 teaspoon dried coriander
1 teaspoon sea salt
1 teaspoon red pepper flakes
1 teaspoon ground cumin

Place all ingredients in a blender or food processor and blend until smooth and creamy. Add water to thin the consistency of the sauce. Transfer the sauce to a pan and gently heat through, keeping warm until ready to serve.

Seitan Vegetables

¼ cup toasted sesame oil
4 garlic cloves, minced or pressed
1 pound seitan, cut into chunks
1 cup broccoli, chopped
1 cup chopped red bell pepper

1 tablespoon sesame seeds
1 teaspoon sea salt
Crushed peanuts to garnish
Chopped fresh cilantro to garnish

Heat the sesame oil in a sauté pan. Add the garlic, seitan, broccoli, red bell pepper, sesame seeds, and salt and cook until vegetables are tender.

Place the seitan vegetables atop the golden rice and drizzle generously with peanut sauce. Sprinkle with the crushed peanuts and fresh cilantro.

• •

OHHHH, PEANUT SAUCE . . . this is highly addictive stuff. You may find yourself dreaming about it, waking up in the middle of the night in a pool of drool. You could experiment with this dish by using other nut butters such as cashew or almond, which are equally enticing. If you're not a huge fan of seitan, try using broccoli or tofu instead or a combination of both. Really, any vegetable will bathe well in the peanut sauce. Make sure you use a seasonal vegetable to get the most flavor out of the dish.

Sean

Tiga-Dega-Na

2 tablespoons peanut oil

1 yellow onion, finely diced

1 tablespoon minced fresh ginger

4 garlic cloves, minced

4 free-range boneless chicken breasts, sliced
   into sixths

Kosher salt and freshly ground black pepper to
   taste

2 tablespoons tomato paste

1 teaspoon cayenne pepper

1 cup tomatoes, peeled, seeded, and diced

1 large yam, diced, with skin left on

2 zucchinis, sliced

1 okra pod, sliced

2 cups chicken stock

1 cup creamy peanut butter

In a large saucepan, heat the peanut oil over medium to high heat. Add the onion and cook, stirring occasionally, until the onion is translucent. Stir in the ginger and garlic and cook for 1 minute more. Add the sliced chicken breast, season with salt and pepper, and slightly brown. Stir in the tomato paste and cayenne pepper and coat the chicken evenly, then add the chopped tomatoes and cubed yam. Simmer for 5 minutes while stirring occasionally, then add the zucchini, okra, and chicken stock. Stir to break up and loosen the dish. Gently simmer for 15 minutes and incorporate the peanut butter. Simmer for another 15 minutes. Serve warm over rice and *geniet*.

• •

IF YOU FIND YOURSELF WALKING on the Ivory Coast and you come across a place called Jioni Anga, open the door, watch your step, sit down at one of the six tables, and order yourself a plate of Tiga-Dega-Na. Actually, I just made that up, but this is one of my all-time favorite dishes, and when Maggie gave me the Seitan Satay I couldn't wait to pair it up with Tiga-Dega-Na.

   This African staple is equally as dreamy and addictive as its Indonesian counterpart. The sauce itself is hardier and, I believe, a welcome change to silky satay-laden menus that have taken over the industry. Also, if you're not a big seitan fan, try using chicken or pork instead.

Maggie

Tempeh Filets with Roasted Beet Chutney

Two 8-ounce tempeh
¼ cup vegetable broth
½ cup soy sauce
¼ cup sherry or dry wine

½ cup minced yellow onion
2 tablespoons olive oil
2 tablespoons horseradish (or more!)
2 tablespoons chopped fresh dill

Place tempeh in a baking dish. Whisk remaining ingredients in a bowl and pour over tempeh. Marinate for 1 hour. Cover the baking dish with foil and bake at 400 degrees for 20 minutes. Uncover, flip tempeh over, and continue baking another 10 minutes until the liquid is evaporated and beginning to caramelize. Serve with Roasted Beet Chutney.

Roasted Beet Chutney

½ cup dried currants or raisins
½ cup hot water
1 pound peeled, chopped chioggia or red beets, green tops removed
1 tart apple, peeled and diced

1 red onion, minced
2 tablespoons olive oil
1 teaspoon caraway seed
1 teaspoon sea salt
2 tablespoons red wine vinegar

Preheat the oven to 400 degrees. Soak currants in hot water for 15 minutes to plump. In a bowl, combine beets, apple, onion, olive oil, caraway seed, and salt and toss well. Place on a baking sheet and cover with foil. Bake for 15 minutes or until beets are tender. Remove from the oven, cool slightly, then transfer to a blender and add soaked currants and vinegar. Pulse the blender until the mixture is well combined but still chunky. Serve at room temperature.

. . . .

THE TEMPEH HERE WAS IN NO WAY meant to compare with Sean's ostrich (thankfully). Trust me, you are not missing out by not chowing down on Sean's unnaturally farm-raised flightless bird. Hundreds of ostrich ranches in the United States have displaced this huge bird from its native lands of Africa and Southwest Asia. Most farms have to use several antibiotics and steroids to maintain the health of the bird in its transplanted environment. The one ingredient that matches up in these side-by-side dishes is the lovely accompaniment of beets. One of the few ingredients about which Sean and I are in complete harmony. Tom Robbins writes about the mystique of beets in his book *Jitterbug Perfume*, making it the essential ingredient in perfume.

Sean

Ostrich Filets with Roasted Beet Relish

1 pound ostrich loin
2 tablespoons port wine
½ teaspoon dried coriander
1 tablespoon whole-grain mustard

1 teaspoon kosher salt
1 teaspoon olive oil
½ cup (4 ounces) chèvre cheese

Cut the ostrich loin into four 4-ounce fillets. In a bowl, thoroughly mix the port wine, coriander, mustard, and salt. Rub the ostrich fillets with the mixture and let marinate for 1 hour. Add the olive oil to a sauté pan over medium to high heat. Sear fillets on each side for about 3 to 5 minutes or until medium rare. Let cool just a bit and spread 2 tablespoons of the chèvre cheese over the top of each fillet. Top with Roasted Beet Relish and enjoy.

Roasted Beet Relish

3 large red beets, green tops removed
2 teaspoons olive oil
2 teaspoons kosher salt
¼ cup finely diced red onion
1 garlic clove, minced

2 tablespoons red wine vinegar
1 tablespoon sugar
2 tablespoons whole-grain mustard
3 tablespoons vegetable oil
Freshly ground black pepper to taste

Preheat the oven to 375 degrees. Coat the beets with the olive oil and 1 teaspoon of the kosher salt. Place on a pan and roast for 1 hour or until the skins start to turn black. Allow the beets to cool completely; then, using a paring knife, remove the skins. It might be wise to wear gloves for this: Dice the peeled beets. Combine the beets and the remaining relish ingredients in a bowl. Combine well and use as desired. The relish can stay in refrigerator for up to one week.

. . . .

IT'S FUNNY HOW MAGGIE is so concerned about the ostrich but not so concerned about the displacement of the soybean from its native land of China. Maybe she just isn't concerned about the life of that little packet of "perfect protein." Also, in today's industry you are going to find more chemicals and pesticides used in the production of soybeans than antibiotics in my heart-healthy bird. And I guarantee that the ostrich loin will be fresher and less processed than the plastic-wrapped hunk of tempeh.

In any case, if you haven't tried ostrich, or you've happened to choose the life of a vegetarian, you really are missing out. Ostrich is a fabulous red meat that is tender, lean, and full of flavor, yet it contains fewer calories and cholesterol than beef, chicken, or pork. Because the meat is so lean it is important not to overcook and dry it out. This is one of the many combinations that will look fantastic next to each other on the dinner table. The beet relish in this recipe is heaven, and so is her chutney. I've never been a big fan of tempeh—clearly not meaty enough—but one day Maggie pulled one over on me and gave me some wonderful-looking barbecue skewers. I should have known something was up by the glint in her eye, but I devoured and delighted in them.

He Said . . .

What follows are the elemental recipes —
with the flair of a carnivore — that I gave
Maggie. Her recipes are the vegetarian
inspirations she responded with.

Earth

Sean

The Carmichael

Four 8-ounce choice beef tenderloin fillets
16 16/20 tiger shrimp, peeled and deveined
4 tablespoons salted sweet cream butter
1 garlic clove, minced

½ cup white wine
1½ cups (12 ounces) Stilton blue cheese, crumbled
Salt and pepper to taste

Preheat the oven to 375 degrees. Grill the steaks to just under the desired doneness. While the steaks are grilling, sauté the shrimp over high heat with the butter and garlic. Deglaze the pan with white wine. Remove the steaks from the grill and cut an "X" in the top of each. Divide the blue cheese between the four steaks and stuff it into the middle of the X. Take four shrimp for each steak and stuff them into the blue cheese with the tails curling over the side of the steak. Place the stuffed steaks on a baking sheet or in a baking dish. Pour the butter and garlic over all. Place in the oven, uncovered, until the cheese is slightly brown and bubbly. Serve right out of the oven and prepare for ecstasy.

• •

OH YEAH, BABY!

You know that wet stuff that's building in the back of your mouth as you read this recipe? That's longing, lust, craving, desire, Pavlov's playdough. Call it what you wish — this steak is the reason that we as a species not only cook but eat.

Don't skimp on the steak. Use a choice cut (preferably Omaha Steaks) and find some fresh shrimp. Really enjoy yourself with this one. And go ahead, share it with some you love — but maybe just a bite or two.

Pair this steak with banana-mashed sweet potatoes, steamed asparagus, and I tell you, if ACDC were there with you, they'd salute you — because you are about to rock.

Pleskac Portobello

**4 large portobello mushrooms (5-inch caps or
     larger)**
Truffle oil
1 cup grated Parmesan cheese
1 cup sour cream
2 tablespoons lemon juice
1 tablespoon dried basil or ¼ cup fresh basil

1 teaspoon fennel seed
1 teaspoon sea salt
1 teaspoon black pepper
1 pound fresh spinach leaves, stems removed
2 cups artichoke hearts, drained and quartered
½ cup finely chopped fresh parsley
1 cup walnut pieces

Preheat the oven to 375 degrees. Remove the
mushroom stems and gently wash the mushroom
caps. Rub the tops with truffle oil and place in a
baking dish with the gill side up. Fill the baking
dish ½ inch deep with lightly sea salted water. Set
aside.

   In a food processor, blend the Parmesan cheese,
sour cream, lemon juice, basil, fennel seed, sea
salt, and pepper until smooth. Transfer to a bowl
and stir in spinach, artichoke hearts, parsley, and
half of the walnuts. Place the mixture into each of
the mushroom caps and top with remaining walnuts. Bake for 25 minutes or until golden and bubbly. Mmmm . . .

· ·

I HESITATED IN USING PORTOBELLO as my vessel since it seems to be the all-too-
common stereotype for steak replacement. The portobello always appears on unimagina-
tive restaurant menus as the token vegetarian option. Often, the overused "Portobello
Burger" ends up truly tasting like a "burger" after occupying the same grill as the juices of
a bloody steak. I use the portobello's shallow cavity to match up to the stuffing technique
in Sean's fillet. Also, the mushroom's similar appearance to steak in color and shape
works for a visual pairing. The truffle oil is a worthy investment since a little drizzle goes a
long way. (And you can use it in the Seitan Stroganoff recipe, too!) Being a known aphrodisiac, the truffle oil will create a dish that entices the meat eaters across the table to sniff
the air in search of that alluring aroma drifting up from your plate.

 Sean

Apple-Brined Chops

4 pork chops, cut at least 2 inches thick
2 quarts water
2 Granny Smith apples, sliced
½ cup dark molasses

1½ cups sea salt
1 tablespoon whole black peppercorns
1 cinnamon stick
1 tablespoon fennel seed

Combine the water, apples, molasses, salt, peppercorns, cinnamon stick, and fennel seed in a pot and bring to a boil. Remove from the heat and cool to room temperature, about a half hour. Strain the liquid and discard the spices and apples. Add the pork chops to the strained liquid and place in the refrigerator for 6 to 12 hours. Heat the grill to a 3-second heat (you can hold your hand above the grate for only 3 seconds). Remove the chops from the brine. Gently pat dry and immediately place on the grill. Grill the chops for 2 minutes, turn 90 degrees, and grill for 2 minutes, flip over and cook for 4 minutes. When the chops are done, transfer to a plate and prepare to worship the juicy sweetness.

TAKE THE TIME TO BRINE! I cannot stress this more. It adds finger-licking moisture, perfectly seasons, and wows everyone every time. It also works well for turkey and shrimp. In the process of brining, the cells let in salty water and then try to equalize the saltiness by letting in more water. The result is a chop that looks like it's about to explode, and one that won't dry out even if you cook it a tad too long. This is also why you should definitely brine your turkey. You can cook that bird to 180 degrees or higher and you will still have juicy meat.

It is important to transfer the chop from the brine right to the grill. You don't want it to sit around and lose all that juicy lusciousness you filled it up with.

Maggie's recipe may save you time and it might even taste good, but it will never attain the depth of flavor the chop achieves.

Tempeh Chop with Apple Chutney

Four 8-ounce tempeh
2 cups vegetable broth
¼ cup molasses
1 tablespoon vegetarian Worcestershire sauce

1 tablespoon minced or pressed garlic
1 tablespoon horseradish
2 teaspoons salt
1 teaspoon black pepper

Preheat the oven to 350 degrees. Arrange the tempeh steaks side by side in a well-oiled baking dish. In a bowl, whisk together vegetable broth, molasses, Worcestershire sauce, garlic, horseradish, salt, and pepper. Pour the liquid over the tempeh and let it marinate at room temperature for 1 hour. Bake, uncovered, for 1 hour until the liquid is absorbed. Flip the tempeh steaks over once halfway through baking time to ensure even baking and even seasoning. Serve with Apple Chutney.

Apple Chutney

¼ cup raisins
½ cup hot water
1 pound apples, peeled and diced
1 tablespoon grated fresh ginger

1 tablespoon vinegar
1 teaspoon five-spice powder
1 teaspoon sea salt

Soak the raisins in the hot water for 10 minutes. In a saucepan combine the soaked raisins in their water, diced apples, grated ginger, vinegar, five-spice powder, and salt. Cover and cook over low heat for 20 to 30 minutes, stirring occasionally.

. . . .

I ADMIRE SEAN'S SLOW APPROACH TO BRINING HIS PIG. My counter-recipe saves time and still produces the same depth of flavor. Five-spice powder is available at most Asian or specialty markets. It is typically used in Chinese cooking and consists of equal parts of clove, fennel seed, Szechuan peppercorns, star anise, and cinnamon. The five-spice powder mimics the spices in Sean's brine but it puts out a more complex and well-rounded flavor in less time. The sweetness in the brined tempeh pairs very nicely with the spicy horseradish. This dish is perfect for winter, with its aroma reminiscent of traditional holiday spice, warming you and infusing your kitchen with a potpourri of enticing smells.

Beef Brisket with Blueberry Barbecue Sauce

One 8-pound brisket, untrimmed
2 yellow onions, coarsely chopped
1½ bottles (18 ounces) beer (any domestic ale)
1 tablespoon kosher salt
5 garlic cloves, peeled
1 bay leaf

2 tablespoons ground cumin
1 tablespoon dried oregano
½ cup brown sugar
1 tablespoon whole black peppercorns
Two 14-ounce cans tomato sauce

Scatter half of the chopped onions on the bottom of a roasting pan. Place the brisket on top of the onions with the fat side up. Pour the beer over the top and sprinkle with the salt. In a food processor, pulse together the remaining onion, the garlic cloves, bay leaf, cumin, oregano, brown sugar, and peppercorns. Add the tomato sauce and blend well. Pour the tomato mixture over the top of the brisket and cover with foil. Bake at 200 degrees for 10 hours. When done, the brisket will be fork tender and will have shrunk by at least three-fourths. Remove from the pan and let sit for 15 minutes. Trim the fat and discard. Remove the tapered end, where the grain runs opposite to the rest of the meat, chop it up, and use it in baked beans or for leftover barbecue sandwiches the next day. Slice the rest, serve warm on a platter blanketed with Blueberry Barbecue Sauce and treasure.

Blueberry Barbecue Sauce

2 tablespoons bacon drippings or butter
1 yellow onion, diced
2 garlic cloves, minced
2 cups tomato sauce
2½ cups fresh blueberries
½ cup water
¼ cup canned chipotles in adobo sauce

1 tablespoon cocoa powder
¼ cup orange juice
¼ cup brown sugar
2 teaspoons dry mustard
2 teaspoons chili powder
Salt and pepper to taste

In a large saucepan over medium heat, sauté the onion and garlic in the bacon drippings until the onions are translucent, about 5 minutes. Add the tomato sauce, 2 cups of the blueberries, water, chipotles, cocoa powder, orange juice, brown sugar, dry mustard, chili powder, salt, and pepper.

Bring the sauce to a boil, then reduce the heat and simmer for 20 to 25 minutes, stirring occasionally. Transfer the sauce to a blender and purée until smooth. Stir in the remaining ½ cup of blueberries and serve warm.

. . . .

THE SLOW, ALL-DAY ROASTING of a large piece of beef is one of the greatest things in the world. From the sound of the dripping juices sizzling as they hit the heat to the mellow smell that envelops your kitchen, it tells you that everything is right with your life, at least for that point in time.

Then, when you start to carve, it is impossible contain yourself. You have to sneak a piece. "For quality control" you tell the person who catches you with a little bit of juice on your chin, and then, with a look of atonement, you offer them a taste of the melt-in-your-mouth ecstasy. Eating a good brisket is a carnivorous orgasm, and it's the one dish that can make any vegetarian question their motives.

Jackfruit Pineapple Barbecue on a Bun

8 whole-grain buns, toasted

Two 20-ounce cans unsweetened jackfruit, drained

1 cup tomato sauce

¼ cup brown sugar

3 tablespoons vegetarian Worcestershire sauce

2 tablespoons apple cider vinegar

2 tablespoons paprika

1 yellow onion, minced

6 garlic cloves, minced or pressed

1 tablespoon ground cumin

1 tablespoon peanut butter

1 tablespoon sea salt

2 teaspoons black pepper

1 teaspoon dried thyme

3 or more dashes of liquid smoke, to taste

Preheat the oven to 350 degrees. In a large bowl, pull apart the jackfruit until evenly shredded or pulse in a food processor until shredded and set aside. Place the remaining ingredients in a food processor and purée until smooth. Pour the sauce over the shredded jackfruit and mix until well coated. Transfer to a shallow baking dish, cover with foil, and bake for 1 hour. Serve on toasted sesame buns.

. . . .

JACKFRUIT HAS TO BE ONE OF MY ALL-TIME FAVORITE meat teasers. It is one of the world's largest fruits, grown in parts of Africa, Brazil, and Southeast Asia. Because of U.S. customs laws, it's only available dried or canned and can be found at most Asian markets. Its young, unripe flavor lies somewhere between hearts of palm and artichoke hearts. When buying canned young jackfruit, make sure it's packed in water only, with no sugar added. Cans of jackfruit also come packed in syrup since it's also eaten as a sweet. When the chunks of jackfruit are pulled apart, the pieces are incredibly similar to shredded pork or beef. After the shreds of jackfruit are coated with a sauce and cooked to absorb the surrounding flavors, it will fool any meat eater. A picnic in the park with these barbecue shredded "meat" sandwiches will leave Sean's leftover brisket sandwiches in the basket. Lay the checkered tablecloth, toast some sesame buns, pass the potato salad, and dig into the most "meaty" fruit ever to go barbecue.

Sean

Moussaka Rocka

8 eggplants
6 tablespoons olive oil
1 pound ground beef
½ pound ground lamb
½ cup all-purpose flour
½ teaspoon kosher salt
Freshly ground black pepper to taste
½ cup chopped mushrooms

½ yellow onion, diced
2 tablespoons butter
1 garlic clove, minced
1 tablespoon tomato purée
1 tablespoon Worcestershire sauce
2 tablespoons chopped pine nuts
2 tablespoons chopped fresh parsley,
2 eggs

Cut 6 of the eggplants in half lengthwise; deeply score the pulp with the tip of a knife. Fry the eggplant halves in 3 tablespoons of the olive oil until the pulp is easily removed with a spoon. Reserve both the skins and the pulp. Brown the beef and lamb and reserve. Peel and thinly slice the other two eggplants. Dredge the slices in the flour seasoned with the salt and pepper and fry in the remaining olive oil. Sauté the mushrooms and onion in the butter until the onion is translucent.

Preheat the oven to 375 degrees. In a bowl, mix together the mushrooms, onion, browned meat, reserved eggplant pulp, garlic, tomato puree, Worcestershire, pine nuts, parsley, eggs, and salt and pepper to taste. Mix thoroughly. In a greased 9 × 13 pan, place half of the fried eggplant skins, then layer with the fried eggplant slices and the meat mixture. Continue layering the eggplant slices and meat mixture. Cover the last layer with the remaining half of the eggplant skins. Bake for 1 hour and let rest for 10 minutes before serving. Serve warm and with love.

· ·

MAGGIE, WHY MUST YOU KEEP GOING ON about baby animals when you have no problem devouring the young life of a broccoli or bean? Is it because you don't hear their howls? What, my friend, will you do when the day comes that we can hear that sweet wee sprout, who is only striving to reach the light of day, cry out, "Why, oh why, must you eat me?" Perhaps your answer will be, "I'm sorry, little one, but within the hierarchical laws of nature I cannot sustain on sunlight and water as perfectly as you, so I must subsist on you and others of your kind. But know I appreciate the energy you are about to provide and take comfort that the laws of nature are also cyclical, so when my life has ended your sort will be supping on me. It's all in *Hamlet*, little bean."

In the meantime, try these recipes side by side. You will see that the addition of meat adds a flavor base that the yogurt can't match, and the fat from the meat gives the defatted sauce some body (or feeling of denseness).

Moussaka Mollie

1 tablespoon olive oil
1 large red onion, sliced very thin
10 garlic cloves, minced
2 cups plain yogurt
4 free-range eggs
1 teaspoon sea salt
2 teaspoons black pepper

½ teaspoon nutmeg
2 cups Great Northern beans, cooked or canned
½ cup capers
½ cup minced fresh parsley
2 pounds eggplant, sliced very thin
1 sliced portobello mushroom, stem removed
4 heirloom tomatoes, sliced in rounds

Preheat the oven to 400 degrees. Sauté the onions and garlic in the olive oil. Set aside to cool. Blend the yogurt, eggs, salt, pepper, and nutmeg in a bowl. Stir in the beans, capers, and parsley. Add the cooled onions and garlic and set the mixture aside. In a well-oiled 9 × 12 baking dish, first layer the eggplant, then alternate layers of the mushrooms and yogurt mixture, finishing with the yogurt mixture and the sliced tomatoes. Cover tightly with foil and bake for 1 hour. Remove the foil and bake for another 10 minutes or until the top is browned. Serve with dollops of plain yogurt and crusty French bread.

· ·

WE ARE NOT CAVE PEOPLE ANYMORE. One need not take the life of another creature to subsist in an earthly survival-of-the-fittest hierarchy. Unlike Sean's recipe, this light and filling vegetarian moussaka has no baby animals and no heaviness from excess fat. The ingredients are simply layered and baked, leaving a clean, fresh taste. Each healthy bite pours down the throat like a faucet from the fountain of youth. The creamy yogurt adds a full, rich, and satisfying flavor without the "feeling of denseness" (unlike the fat-laden body of Sean's moussaka).

Sean

Shepherd's Pie with Welsh Rabbit

1 small yellow onion, diced
7 tablespoons butter
2 tablespoons all-purpose flour
⅓ cup beef stock or broth
1½ pounds leftover pot roast, chopped
1 large carrot, diced
½ cup fresh sweet peas
1 leaf fresh sage, chiffonade

Salt and black pepper to taste
1½ pounds red potatoes, quartered, with skins
   left on
½ cup sour cream
¼ cup milk
½ cup beer (any domestic ale)
¾ cup (6 ounces) shredded cheddar cheese
4 large slices of crusty bread

Over medium heat, cook the onion in 2 tablespoons of the butter until translucent. Add the flour and mix thoroughly. Slowly stir in the beef stock. Add the pot roast, carrot, peas, sage, salt, and pepper. Simmer for 3 minutes. Transfer to a shallow baking dish and cool completely. Boil the potatoes, drain, and mash with 4 tablespoons of the butter, sour cream, and milk; set aside.

Preheat the oven to 400 degrees. When the meat mixture has cooled and "set up" (if it's not firm the mashed potatoes will sink into it), spread the mashed potatoes over the top evenly with a fork. Top with the remaining 1 tablespoon of butter and bake for 30 minutes.

In a saucepan, bring the beer to a boil. Reduce the heat and slowly whisk in the shredded cheese. Drizzle the Shepherd's Pie with the Welsh Rabbit and serve with bread. Enjoy.

• •

THIS ENTRÉE, I HAVE TO ADMIT, is a stick-to-your-ribs, slow-down-the-flow meal. But, man, meat and potatoes with a rich cheese and beer sauce — you just have to indulge once in a while.

I should explain that the Welsh Rabbit is not a typo. It is a dish that is traditionally served over bread and technically called "rarebit," but because of the wonderfully beautiful Welsh accent it comes out "rabbit."

It's funny how Maggie is all concerned with semantics and traditions now. Yes, lamb and mutton was used quite often with this dish, but it's truly a creation of the total utilization philosophy, being a cheap way to revive leftover Sunday roast. For this reason I use leftover pot roast rather than fresh young sheep.

Maggie

Gardener's Pie

1 pound unpeeled Yukon Gold or red potatoes, diced
½ pound unpeeled turnips, diced
½ cup soy milk
1 tablespoon nutritional yeast
1 tablespoon garlic powder
1 tablespoon onion powder
1 teaspoon sea salt
1 teaspoon black pepper
1 tablespoon olive oil
6 garlic cloves, minced or pressed

1 yellow onion, minced
1 cup diced carrot
2 teaspoons thyme
1 teaspoon sea salt
1 teaspoon black pepper
1 cup sliced mushrooms
1 cup fresh or frozen peas
½ cup bulgur wheat
½ cup white wine or vegetable broth
¼ cup soy sauce
¼ cup fresh parsley to garnish

Preheat the oven to 400 degrees. In a large stockpot, boil the potatoes and turnips in salted water until tender. Drain and combine with soy milk, nutritional yeast, garlic powder, onion powder, salt, and pepper. Beat with an electric mixer until light and fluffy. Set aside. Heat the olive oil in a sauté pan. Add the garlic, onion, carrots, thyme, salt, and pepper. Sauté until the onions are soft; then add mushrooms, peas, and bulgur wheat. Stir to marry the flavors; then add the wine or broth and the soy sauce. Continue cooking until all the liquid is absorbed. Pour the mixture in a baking pan and top with mashed potato and turnip mixture. Bake, uncovered, for 15 to 20 minutes or until potato peaks are golden brown. Garnish with fresh parsley.

. . . .

THIS TRADITIONAL BRITISH RECIPE is called Shepherd's Pie when made with lamb. The name of the dish changes to Cottage Pie when made with beef and Fishermen's Pie when made with seafood. To keep with namesake tradition, I have called this one Gardener's Pie. It's a hearty and satisfying comfort food. In my vegetarian opinion, there's absolutely no need for lamb or mutton in this historical dish. What loving shepherd would slay his wool-providing flock of companions for a meal? This compassionate version of Shepherd's Pie ensures all the warmth, nutrition, and filling comfort without any blood-shed. Combining turnips with potatoes in the mashed topping gives it added flavor, as does the cheeselike taste of nutritional yeast powder. The nutritional yeast powder is an excellent source of protein and complex B vitamins. The peas and carrots make this quite colorful, but feel free to experiment with other vegetables like corn or peppers.

Water

Sean

Saffron Poached Tilapia Painted with Balsamic Syrup and Basil Oil

4 tilapia fillets
2 cups water
½ cup Chablis

3 saffron stigmas (or threads)
1 tablespoon salted sweet cream butter
Salt and pepper to taste

Lay the tilapia, skin side down, in a straight-sided sauté pan and add the water, wine, saffron, butter, salt, and pepper. Cover and simmer for 5 to 7 minutes. Carefully transfer to plate and drizzle Balsamic Syrup and Basil Oil over the top.

Balsamic Syrup

1 cup balsamic vinegar
2 tablespoons sugar

1 teaspoon cornstarch
1 tablespoon water

In a saucepot mix the vinegar and sugar and cook until reduced by half. Mix the cornstarch in the water and whisk it into the reduced vinegar to thicken. Simmer for five minutes and served chilled.

Basil Oil

½ cup olive oil

⅓ cup fresh basil leaves

In a stainless steel pot over a low flame, heat the basil and olive oil together. Allow it to cool and infuse for 1 day, then strain before use.

· ·

MAD ABOUT SAFFRON? QUITE RIGHTLY!

This pungent little spice, which is actually the stigma of a flower, just pulls at my breadbasket threads. I think it is the whole romance that gets me. Fields of purple crocuses and singing Italian women picking the stigmas out of the flowers. Well, who knows.

Saffron has a slightly earthy flavor that works well with the subtle nuttiness of the tilapia. It creates an eye-popping entrée with a mellow yellow glow that completes the dish, making it attractive to all the senses. It is this hue and its medicinal qualities that have made saffron one of the most sought-after and fought-over spices throughout the ages.

Don't let the artistic beauty of this dish scare you like it did Maggie. It's easy and can be made any time you want a little color and pizzazz to liven your day. You won't have to save it for a special occasion like Maggie's "labor of love" — you can just love it and leave the labor to the people who really do have to wear "starched chef jackets." To liven things up, serve the fish alongside roasted purple fingerling potatoes and coconut cabbage slaw.

And hey, if you are going to eat cholesterol-riddled eggs rather than this heart-healthy fish, eat a steak.

Saffron Poached Tofu on Fennel Bruschetta with Avgolemono Sauce

Poached Tofu

Two 12-ounce packages of extra-firm silken tofu, cut in 4 halves
2 cups water
½ cup white wine

½ teaspoon saffron threads, crushed
1 fennel bulb with fronds, cut in half
2 teaspoons sea salt

Slice the tofu into 8 slabs equal in size. In a 2-quart sauté pan, bring tofu, water, wine, saffron, fennel, and sea salt to a boil. Cover and simmer for 15 minutes. With a slotted spoon, remove the fennel and set aside for the bruschetta.

Bruschetta

8 slices of Italian bread, toasted
Boiled fennel (from poaching liquid)
1 tablespoon olive oil

Salt and black pepper to taste
Several leaves of fresh spinach

Purée the fennel and the olive oil to a smooth paste. Add salt and pepper to taste. Spread on the slices of toasted Italian bread. Place the bruschetta on a bed of fresh spinach leaves. Top each bruschetta with a slice of tofu and drizzle with Avgolemono Sauce.

Avgolemono Sauce

One 12-ounce package of extra-firm silken tofu
⅓ cup lemon juice
2 tablespoons vegetable broth powder
1 tablespoon soy sauce
1 tablespoon onion powder
2 teaspoons garlic powder

2 teaspoons honey
½ teaspoon turmeric
½ teaspoon ground nutmeg
½ teaspoon sea salt
¼ teaspoon white pepper

Place all ingredients in a blender and process until very smooth. Transfer to a saucepan and heat thoroughly. Serve warm.

. . . .

THIS IS ONE OF THE FIRST RECIPES Sean gave me to contend with. I thought it was over the top with his "balsamic syrup" and "basil oil," so I decided I would take this matching recipe to his starched-chef-jacket level. You may want to save this dish for a special occasion, since it is a labor of love. But if you have the time and the creative edge, then it's a really fun dish to make. The soft silken texture of the tofu is akin to the poached white of an egg. A traditional avgolemono sauce is a Greek lemon sauce that is made with egg yolks and chicken stock. If you wish to make this dish with organic free-range eggs instead of tofu, then you may want to authenticate the sauce as well.

To poach eggs, bring poaching liquid close to, but not at, boiling (200 degrees). The water should "shiver" but no air bubbles should break on the surface. Break the eggs into a bowl one at a time and carefully slide the egg from the bowl into the water and simmer them 3 minutes or until soft to the touch. Gently remove the eggs with a slotted spoon.

Sean

Grilled Salmon alla Piccata

Four 8-ounce salmon fillets, skin removed
2 garlic cloves, minced
8 large mushrooms, sliced thinly
1 teaspoon olive oil
1 cup white wine
⅓ cup capers

½ teaspoon kosher salt
Freshly ground black pepper to taste
½ cup fish stock
½ cup freshly squeezed lemon juice
¼ cup heavy whipping cream
Zest of 1 lemon

Grill the salmon to your preferred doneness. Sauté the garlic and mushrooms in the olive oil. Deglaze pan with the white wine. Add capers, salt, pepper, and fish stock and reduce by half. Add the lemon juice and whipping cream and reduce by half again. Add the lemon zest and drape the sauce over the salmon fillets. *Pásatelo bien.*

· ·

" I HAVE A FEELING MAGGIE COULDN'T MATCH a recipe resembling the Salmon alla Piccata because she realizes its flawlessness. The lemony tang exquisitely cleaving the buttery oil of the salmon — I'm speculating she can't think about this recipe without longing for a nibble or two. She has to resort to her friend the eggplant and smother it with tomatoes and cheese to try and move her desires back in line with her convictions.

SERVES 4 TO 6

Grilled Eggplant alla Caprese

2 eggplants, cut in ½-inch-thick slices
2 tablespoons olive oil
2 tablespoons crushed garlic
4 heirloom tomatoes, sliced
1 pound fresh mozzarella cheese, sliced

1 cup fresh basil leaves, loosely packed, plus a few leaves for garnish
Salt and pepper to taste
Balsamic vinegar to drizzle (optional)

Combine the olive oil and garlic and brush on both sides of the eggplant slices. Grill the eggplant until slightly charred. In a baking dish, layer half of the grilled eggplant slices and half of the tomatoes, mozzarella, and basil. Sprinkle the salt and pepper between each layer. Repeat layers with the remaining half. Place under the broiler until the cheese is browned. Garnish with fresh basil and drizzle with a splash of balsamic vinegar.

. . . .

SO THIS ISN'T A PERFECT MATCH to Sean's challenge, but when it's made at the peak of the summer season, this dish is unbelievable. It is crucial that the tomatoes and eggplant are at their ripest, since there is no heavy seasoning or sauce to mask their flavor. This has to be one of the easiest meals to make. Use fresh, Italian-style mozzarella cheese that comes packed in whey or water. I recommend using buffalo mozzarella for a sweet, delicate flavor.

# Sean

Pan-Seared Tuna with Wasabi Aioli

4 ahi (yellowfin) tuna steaks, 1 inch thick
1 teaspoon olive oil

½ teaspoon kosher salt

Coat the bottom of a cast-iron skillet or heavy frying pan with the olive oil. Set it on a high flame and allow enough time for it to get really hot. Sprinkle the salt over the tuna. Sear the tuna steaks for 2 minutes on each side. (This amount of time pro- duces a rare to medium rare steak; for a more done steak, cover the pan and increase the time. Plate while still warm and serve with a dollop of wasabi aioli. Enjoy.

Wasabi Aioli

1 garlic clove
½ teaspoon kosher salt
1 egg yolk

1½ tablespoons wasabi paste
Juice of 1 lemon
1 cup olive oil

In a mortar, pound the garlic and salt to form a paste. Add the egg yolk, wasabi paste, and lemon juice and mix thoroughly. Stir in the olive oil in a slow trickle against the side of the mortar until completely combined. Chill. The wasabi aioli can stay in your refrigerator for 1 week.

• •

THIS DISH IS QUITE SIMPLY A JOY TO EAT. It is quick to prepare and has a pleasingly lingering affect on the taste buds' memory. Give the dish a try at medium rare and pair it with fried chasoba noodles and gingered carrots. I think you'll find it a worthwhile adventure.

I too am appalled at the amount of heavy metals found in the large and tastier fish. It's a shame we as sentient beings have let the pollution of our planet get so out of hand. I don't want to get off on a rant, so take advantage of Maggie's cleansing nori and recycle your Sunday papers.

Pan-Fried Tofu with Silken Wasabi Sauce

One 12-ounce package silken tofu
2 tablespoons wasabi paste
2 tablespoons mirin or rice wine
2 tablespoons water

1 tablespoon lemon juice
1 tablespoon soy sauce
1 teaspoon garlic powder

Tofu

1 pound hard tofu
¼ cup soy sauce

2 sheets of toasted nori seaweed
1 cup peanut oil

Purée all the ingredients for the Silken Wasabi Sauce in a food processor until smooth and creamy. Set aside. Cut the tofu in four ½-inch-thick slabs. Drizzle soy sauce on the tofu and let stand for 10 minutes to absorb. Cut 2-inch strips from the long side of the nori sheet. Wrap the strips around the tofu, using a dab of water to seal the nori in place. Heat the peanut oil in a skillet on medium-high heat. Carefully slide the slabs of wrapped tofu into the hot oil and fry until golden on both sides. Remove the tofu with a slotted spoon and place on paper towels to absorb the excess oil. Serve with Silken Wasabi Sauce.

• •

THIS RECIPE CONTAINS ALL THE FLAVOR of the sea without the high mercury levels found in Sean's tuna. The nori seaweed strips on the tofu matches the seafood taste of Sean's toxic fish. In fact, seaweed actually removes heavy metals and radioactive elements from the body. So those dining on Sean's plate might want to steal a bite or two from their partner's vegetarian plate to help cleanse their bodies. This dish is a fantastic follow-up to sushi appetizers.

Sean

Grilled Halibut on Nutty Rice

4 fresh halibut fillets, 6 ounces each
½ cup fish stock
½ teaspoon rice wine vinegar

Dash sesame oil
Dash cayenne pepper
Sea salt and black pepper to taste

Nutty Rice

2¼ cups water
1 cup brown rice
1 teaspoon sea salt
1 tablespoon minced fresh garlic
½ teaspoon olive oil

2 tablespoons thinly sliced red onion
¼ cup thinly sliced red bell pepper
¼ cup thinly sliced green bell pepper
¼ cup thinly sliced yellow bell pepper
¼ cup chopped roasted peanuts (unsalted)

Dressing

1½ tablespoons balsamic vinegar
1½ tablespoons soy sauce
2 tablespoons honey

Dash cayenne pepper
1½ tablespoons sesame oil

Preheat the oven to 375 degrees. Place the halibut fillets in a shallow baking dish and add the fish stock. Drizzle the fillets with the rice wine vinegar and sesame oil and season with the cayenne pepper, salt, and black pepper. Bake, covered with aluminum foil, for 15 minutes or until the fish is cooked through. Transfer the halibut to a dish and chill completely.

For the Nutty Rice, bring the water to a rolling boil, then add the brown rice and reduce the heat to a slow simmer. Stir, cover, and simmer until most of the liquid has been absorbed (20 minutes). Stir in the salt and minced garlic. Remove from the heat and keep the rice covered until all the liquid has been absorbed. In a sauté pan over high heat, sauté the onion and bell peppers in the olive oil until the onions are translucent. Remove from the heat and set aside.

To make the dressing, combine the balsamic vinegar, soy sauce, honey, and cayenne pepper in a bowl. Slowly whisk in the sesame oil.

In a bowl, combine the rice, dressing, sautéed vegetables, and peanuts and mix thoroughly. Cool completely before serving. Serve the chilled halibut over the chilled rice and enjoy.

THIS IS ONE OF THOSE SEASONAL MEAT ENTRÉES, according to Maggie, that we rapacious flesh eaters aren't able to enjoy. Have this cool meal on a blazing summer's day with a nice Moscato, and the dusk will shift to passionate conversations and fervent Scrabble competitions.

Maggie

Tofu Ceviche on Sesame Black Rice

2 pounds firm tofu

1 cup lime juice

¼ cup minced scallions

¼ cup finely chopped fresh cilantro

2 tablespoons minced celery

2 tablespoons minced red bell pepper

2 tablespoons grated carrot

1 tablespoon toasted nori, crumbled to small
  sprinkles

1 jalapeño, seeded and minced

1 teaspoon vegetarian Worcestershire sauce

Salt and black pepper to taste

4 cups water

1 tablespoon salt

2 cups Chinese black rice

4 garlic cloves

2 tablespoons toasted sesame oil

Sesame seeds to garnish

For the Tofu Ceviche, drain and squeeze out any extra water from the tofu. Dice tofu in ½-inch cubes and toss gently with the lime juice, scallions, cilantro, celery, red bell pepper, carrot, nori, jalapeño, vegetarian Worcestershire sauce, salt, and pepper. Cover and marinate in the refrigerator for 4 hours or overnight.

For the Nutty Rice, bring the water and salt to a boil. Add the Chinese black rice and the garlic. Cover and simmer 30 minutes or until the water is absorbed and the rice is tender. Stir in the toasted sesame oil and chill. Serve cold. Spread the rice over the plates and top with Tofu Ceviche. Garnish with sesame seeds.

. . . .

THIS VEGETARIAN VERSION OF CEVICHE has a zesty fresh flavor that is similar to pico de gallo. The nori seaweed adds that fishlike flavor of the sea without the bacterial risks of raw fish. I use white tofu to pair up to the white flesh of the overfished heavy-metal halibut that Sean uses.

Sean

Duck Breast Stuffed Trout

4 fresh, whole brook trout, with heads still on
1 boneless duck breast, fat and skin trimmed
2 tablespoons sesame oil
1 pound Swiss chard, chopped
1 tablespoon lemon juice

4 fresh thyme sprigs
8 large grape leaves
Kosher salt and freshly ground black pepper to
    taste

Preheat the oven to 350 degrees. Rub the duck breast with ½ teaspoon of the sesame oil. Sprinkle with salt and either bake or grill the duck breast to medium rare. Dice the cooked duck and combine with the Swiss chard and lemon juice in a bowl. Divide the duck mixture into fourths. Stuff the cavity of each trout with the duck mixture and a sprig of thyme. Coat the trout with the remaining sesame oil, salt, and pepper and wrap each trout in two grape leaves. Place the stuffed trout in a baking dish. Bake until the internal temperature reaches 120 degrees, about 9 to 12 minutes. Serve warm and catch a thrill.

· ·

DON'T MAKE THAT FACE. Not until you've tried it. Duck and trout may seem like unlikely partners, but their qualities combine to form a perfect union. The fat — yes, the fat — of the duck permeates the dish and embellishes the trout's inherent flavor. It may make some diners squeamish to leave the head on the fish, but I believe that you, as a carnivore, should be capable of looking your meal in the eye. Honestly, if you can't consider, and be thankful for, the being that you are consuming, you should seriously ponder switching to nuts and berries.

Maggie's match to this recipe would make the perfect side to this dish, so make them both and eat them together. The pouty vegetarians will just have to have some understanding while you indulge in a gastronomic gala and they scrounge for a nondairy butter substitute to slather on their muffin.

Maggie

Pinto Vegetable Stuffed Cornbread

Cornbread Muffins

1 cup organic unbleached flour
1 cup organic cornmeal
2 teaspoons baking powder
1 teaspoon baking soda
1 teaspoon sea salt

1 teaspoon red pepper flakes
½ teaspoon ground cumin
½ teaspoon dried thyme
1⅓ cups organic milk or soy milk
1 free-range egg

Pinto Vegetable Stuffing

1 white or yellow onion, minced
1 tablespoon garlic, minced or pressed
1 jalapeño, minced and seeded
2 teaspoons cumin seed
1 teaspoon sea salt
1 teaspoon black pepper
2 tablespoons corn oil
¼ cup each red and green bell pepper

¼ cup fresh or frozen corn
2 cups pinto beans, cooked or canned
½ cup chopped heirloom tomatoes
¼ pound chopped Swiss chard
Juice of 1 lime
¼ cup finely chopped fresh cilantro
1 cup sour cream (optional)

Preheat the oven to 375 degrees. In a bowl, sift together the flour, cornmeal, baking powder, baking soda, salt, pepper flakes, cumin, and thyme. In another bowl, whisk together the milk and egg. Add the milk and egg to the dry ingredients and stir until just combined — *do not overmix*. The batter will be slightly lumpy. Pour into a greased, extra-large-sized 6-muffin tin. Bake for 25 minutes. Cool completely. Using a paring knife, cut a hollow cavity in each muffin, thereby creating a cup for the filling.

For the filling, combine the onions, garlic, jala-peño, and cumin seed and sprinkle with the salt and pepper. Heat the corn oil in a sauté pan and sauté until the onions are translucent and the cumin seeds pop. Add bell peppers, corn, pinto beans, tomatoes, and Swiss chard. Cover and cook for 10 minutes. Remove from the heat and add the lime juice.

Fill the cornbread muffins with the hot filling and garnish with fresh cilantro and dollops of sour cream.

. . . .

ASIDE FROM THE FACT that they are both stuffed dishes, these two recipes share nothing in common. Sean's strange combination of mixing creatures of the water and air into a single dish is not something I wanted to recreate. Instead, I chose to blend flavors that have more in common. The spiced cornbread pairs perfectly with the pinto bean mixture. Sean's Duck Breast Stuffed Trout is just wrong. A fish in a bird?

Wind

Sean

SERVES 4

Fig Stuffed Game Hens

4 Cornish game hens, thawed
1 tablespoon melted butter
¼ cup honey
¼ cup balsamic vinegar
1 tablespoon kosher salt

Freshly ground black pepper to taste
⅓ cup port wine
3 sliced fresh black mission figs, stems removed
2 tablespoons heavy whipping cream

The Stuffin'
6 fresh Calimyrna figs, chopped
1 small Vidalia onion, diced
1 garlic clove, minced

½ teaspoon chopped fresh winter savory
½ cup (4 ounces) chèvre cheese, crumbled
½ cup breadcrumbs (panko or Italian)

Preheat the oven to 400 degrees. In a bowl combine the stuffin' ingredients and mix well. Divide the stuffing into fourths and stuff each hen. In a small bowl combine the melted butter, honey, and balsamic vinegar. Mix well. Place the bird breast side up on a rack in a shallow roasting pan. Using a brush, lightly coat each hen with some of the honey mixture. Sprinkle with the salt and pepper and roast, uncovered, for 45 minutes. During the last 15 minutes baste regularly with the remaining honey mixture. When the time is up, transfer the hens to a platter and place the roasting pan on the stove over medium heat. To make the sauce: Deglaze the pan with the port wine. Add the figs and whipping cream and reduce by two-thirds. Drizzle the sauce over the plattered fowl.

IF YOU FIND IT HARD TO GET, or to flip the bill for, fresh figs then dried could be substituted here. I don't know that I would recommend it, though. The fresh fig has a resonance and earthiness that the sweeter dried version tends to lose. Also, there is a rising trend to once again pair figs with blue cheese. It is an amazing combination that you should try, though not here. The blue cheese would overpower the creamy sweetness of the stuffing.

Pay no mind to Maggie's talk of astringent vinegar; in this case I'm not sure she knows what she's talking about. Also, if you add a little salt or butter to Ms. P's squash it will enhance the flavors and round out the base, like I'm always talking about.

Maggie

Fig and Orzo Stuffed Acorn Squash

2 acorn squashes, cut in half, seeds removed
1 tablespoon olive oil
3 Vidalia onions, chopped
3 garlic cloves, minced or pressed
1 cup orzo pasta
1 cup water with 1 teaspoon salt added

6 fresh figs, chopped in small pieces
1 cup toasted walnuts
1 cup chèvre cheese
¼ cup capers
½ cup minced fresh parsley

Preheat the oven to 400 degrees. Place the squash halves cavity side down in a large baking pan. Fill the pan with salted water 1 to 2 inches deep. Bake, uncovered, 40 minutes or until tender to the touch.

For the stuffin': Sprinkle onions and garlic with salt and sauté in olive oil until softened. Add the orzo and sauté another 5 minutes. Add the salted water and bring to a boil; reduce to a simmer. Cook the orzo until the water is absorbed and the orzo is tender (add water if necessary). Remove from the heat. Stir in the figs, walnuts, chévre, capers, and half the parsley.

Fill the cavity of the squash with the stuffing and garnish with the remaining parsley.

. . . .

I DECIDED TO TAKE ON SEAN'S CHALLENGE by matching the method of stuffing rather than the ingredient base. Winter squash is one of those vegetables that loves to be stuffed. When creating the cavity, save the seeds either to toast for a tasty snack or replant in next year's garden. The seeds are nice to save for future breeds of open-pollinated squash. The hollowed-out acorn squash makes a unique bowl for soup. Unlike Sean's feathered stuffing, the inherent flavor of the squash stands alone. The sweet orange flesh doesn't need the addition of syrupy honey or astringent vinegar. The indirect use of salt enhances the edible bowl, which will also disappear by the end of the meal.

Sean

Strawberry Marinated Chicken Breast with Mole

Four 8-ounce boneless free-range chicken
  breasts
1 pint fresh strawberries, sliced
2 tablespoons sugar

1 tablespoon freshly ground black peppercorns
¼ cup white wine
1 tablespoon lime juice
½ teaspoon lime zest

Combine the strawberries, sugar, ground peppercorns, white wine, lime juice, and lime zest in a food processor. Pulse twice. Pour the strawberry mixture over the top of the chicken and let it marinate, in the refrigerator, for a half hour.

Preheat the oven to 425 degrees. In a greased baking dish, bake the marinated chicken for 35 minutes or until its internal temperature reaches 160 degrees. Let the chicken rest and transfer it to a serving platter. Serve with warm mole.

Mole

¼ cup black sesame seeds
½ cup slivered almonds
1 dried chili pepper
1 large yellow onion, chopped
3 garlic cloves, minced
⅓ cup raisins
2 tablespoons chili powder
½ teaspoon ground coriander
¼ teaspoon ground cloves

¼ teaspoon ground fennel seed
1 cinnamon stick
One 14-ounce can diced tomatoes
2 cups water
¼ cup tomato paste
1 cube chicken bouillon
3 ounces unsweetened Mexican chocolate,
  chopped

Toast the sesame seeds in a small, hot frying pan until golden brown. Remove from the pan and set aside. Put the almonds in the pan and toast them to a golden brown; remove and set aside. Put the chili pepper in the pan and heat until it is softened well; remove and set aside.

  In a saucepan, combine the onion, garlic, raisins, chili powder, coriander, cloves, fennel seed, cinnamon stick, and the reserved toasted sesame seeds,

almonds, and chili pepper. Pour in the tomatoes and water. Stir in the tomato paste and the chicken bouillon. Cover and cook on low heat for 2 hours, checking and stirring frequently.

  Remove the cinnamon stick and the stem of the chili pepper. Using an immersion blender, or in a food processor, blend until smooth. Add the chocolate and stir until well incorporated. Serve warm over the chicken and enjoy.

• •

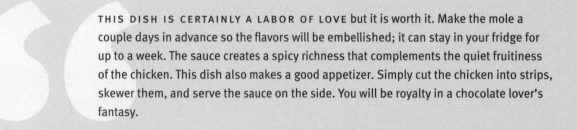

THIS DISH IS CERTAINLY A LABOR OF LOVE but it is worth it. Make the mole a couple days in advance so the flavors will be embellished; it can stay in your fridge for up to a week. The sauce creates a spicy richness that complements the quiet fruitiness of the chicken. This dish also makes a good appetizer. Simply cut the chicken into strips, skewer them, and serve the sauce on the side. You will be royalty in a chocolate lover's fantasy.

Mole Marinated Tempeh with Strawberry Avocado Salsa

Four 8-ounce tempeh

Preheat the oven to 375 degrees. Slice each tempeh in half. Place 4 slices of the halved tempeh in a well-oiled baking dish and cover with half the mole. Layer remaining 4 tempeh halves on top and cover with the remaining mole. Bake, covered, for 1 hour. Serve topped with salsa.

Mole

¼ cup toasted sesame seeds
¼ cup toasted pumpkin seeds
1 dried chipotle pepper or 1 tablespoon chipotle powder
1 yellow onion
2 tablespoons garlic, minced or pressed
2 teaspoons sea salt

1 teaspoon black pepper
1 teaspoon cinnamon
1 teaspoon chili powder
¼ teaspoon ground cumin
2 cups chopped tomatoes
3 tablespoons unsweetened cocoa powder

Purée all mole ingredients in a food processor and process until smooth.

Salsa

2 avocados
1 cup fresh organic strawberries
1 red onion

2 tablespoons vinegar
1 teaspoon sea salt
½ cup minced fresh cilantro

Cut avocados in half, remove the pits, and carefully scoop out the flesh, leaving it intact. Finely dice the avocado, strawberries, and onion and toss together with the vinegar, salt, and cilantro.

. . . .

IF YOU WERE FORTUNATE ENOUGH to find cocoa nibs at your local specialty store, I encourage you to substitute 3 ounces of nibs for the 3 tablespoons of unsweetened cocoa powder. Cocoa nibs are broken bits of roasted cacao beans and have a very intense flavor that range from smoky to fruity. They are lovely.

Sean

Turkey Zucchini Casserole

1 pound ground turkey

6 medium to large zucchini, sliced very thin lengthwise

1 teaspoon sesame oil

1 garlic clove, minced

1 teaspoon dried basil

1 teaspoon dried oregano

1 teaspoon freshly ground fennel seed

Kosher salt and freshly ground black pepper to taste

½ cup white wine

¼ cup heavy whipping cream

¼ cup lemon juice

½ cup breadcrumbs

½ red onion, sliced thin

1 tablespoon fresh basil leaves, chiffonade

In a large skillet, brown the ground turkey in the sesame oil with the minced garlic, dried basil, oregano, fennel seed, salt, pepper, and just a dash of the white wine. Set aside to cool before assembling.

In a bowl combine the rest of the wine with the whipping cream and lemon juice; whip slightly. Grease the bottom of a 9 × 13 casserole dish and arrange in it a layer of sliced zucchini, making sure that the slices overlap. Spread a thin layer of the seasoned ground turkey on top of the zucchini and distribute over it some of the red onion, bread crumbs, and fresh basil. Drizzle over that a small amount of the wine and cream mixture, season with some salt and pepper, and top with another layer of overlapping zucchini slices. Repeat this process 2 more times.

Pour the remaining wine and cream mixture over the top, cover with foil, and allow the casserole to rest in the fridge for about 30 minutes. Preheat the oven to 375 degrees. Cover and bake the casserole for 50 minutes; uncover and bake 10 more minutes. Serve warm and live to the fullest.

• •

I INCLUDED THIS RECIPE IN HOMAGE to the late Sue Rosowski, who with her husband, Jim, loved this casserole and ordered it often during the summer months. It's a surprisingly light dish that doesn't weigh you down, allowing those half light strolls in search of deer or pheasant.

For an interesting twist on the breadcrumbs, use crushed frosted flakes. The sweet and salty combination earns rave reviews when used as a topping or a coating for fried chicken. If you are not up for the adventure or want a more traditional homey feel, use fried onions.

Jackfruit Zucchini Casserole

Two 20-ounce cans unsweetened jackfruit,
   drained and shredded
2 teaspoons olive oil
2 teaspoons garlic, minced or pressed
1 teaspoon dried oregano
1 teaspoon dried basil
1 teaspoon salt
1 teaspoon black pepper

½ cup vegetable broth
2 tablespoons white wine
6 zucchinis, sliced lengthwise
¾ cup panko or other breadcrumbs
¾ cup soy milk
3 tablespoons soy sauce
1 tablespoon nutritional yeast

Preheat the oven 375 degrees. Brown the shredded jackfruit in the olive oil along with the garlic, oregano, basil, salt, and pepper. Add the vegetable broth and white wine and continue to cook until all the liquid is gone.

   In a well-oiled baking dish, layer the zucchini slices, making sure that the slices overlap.

Alternate with the cooked jackfruit and panko. Repeat the layers, ending at the top with the panko. Mix together the soy milk, soy sauce, and nutritional yeast and pour over the top of the casserole. Bake, covered, for 45 minutes. Uncover and bake for 15 more minutes to crisp the top.

. . . .

JACKFRUIT IS AN AMAZING POULTRY SUBSTITUTE. The appearance and texture is so similar to Sean's bird flesh that the two dishes side by side would be hard to tell apart. With the similar seasonings, you could fool the meat eater into thinking you actually made the Turkey Zucchini Casserole instead. Panko is a type of breadcrumb often used in Japanese cooking for coating fried foods. If you can't find panko, any breadcrumbs will do. Or you might try crushed crackers for an interesting topping. As for Sean's cereal idea, cornflakes maybe, but frosted flakes, seriously? Your best bet is to save your cereal for the breakfast bowl.

Sean

SERVES 4

Penne Puttanesca with Roasted Quail

Roasted Quail

½ cup red wine
2 tablespoons olive oil
2 tablespoons dried basil

¼ cup molasses
4 young quail, with breast bone removed
1 teaspoon kosher salt

Combine the red wine, olive oil, basil, and molasses in a bowl. Rinse the quail and pat dry with a paper towel. Place the quail in a shallow pan and pour the wine and molasses mixture over them. Sprinkle the salt over the top of the birds and marinate for 30 minutes to an hour.

Preheat the oven to 450 degrees. Transfer the quail from the marinade to a rack inside a roasting pan. Roast for 15 minutes or until done.

Penne Puttanesca

1 pound dry penne pasta
1 teaspoon olive oil
One 2-ounce can anchovy fillets, chopped fine
1 medium shallot, minced
2 cloves of garlic, minced
2 tablespoons large capers, drained and rinsed
¼ cup kalamata olives, pitted and chopped fine
¼ cup green olives, pitted and chopped fine

½ pound baby zucchini, sliced
½ cup dry white wine
1 tablespoon red pepper flakes
Kosher salt and freshly ground pepper to taste
1 pound can whole tomatoes, chopped with the juice, seeds and all
6 fresh basil leaves, chiffonade

Bring 6 quarts of water to a boil and add 2 tablespoons of salt. Drop in the penne pasta and boil for approximately 18 minutes or until the pasta is al dente.

In a large skillet heat the olive oil over medium to high heat. Add the anchovy fillets and shallot and sauté until the shallots are translucent. Add the garlic and capers and sauté for 1 minute more. Toss in the kalamata and green olives and the zucchini. Deglaze the pan with the white wine and season with the pepper flakes, salt, and pepper. Turn down the fire to a medium heat. Reduce the mixture by half and add the tomatoes and tomato juice; season again. Reduce by half again.

Drain the pasta and toss it in the sauce along with the fresh basil. Serve the pasta in a large bowl with the roasted quail on top.

• •

PUTTANESCA IS A PHENOMENALLY FLAVORFUL SAUCE that is simple to make. It stands up well with any meat from fish to emus or is enough of a "main course" to be a quick meal after work. Some might think, looking at the recipe, that the sauce will come out too salty or fishy, but the acid from the tomatoes level the sauce out, and the anchovies dissolve into the undertones heightened by the refreshing fire of the pepper flakes. Maggie, unfortunately, loses this undertone in her pink tomato sauce that, with the addition of her creamy cheese, actually comes out a bit more hardy than the puttanesca she considers robust. Though I think her quarkie sauce is good, it's no puttanesca.

Penne Puttanesca with Quark

2 tablespoons garlic, minced or pressed
1 shallot, minced
1 teaspoon olive oil
2 tablespoons capers
¼ cup kalamata olives, pitted and chopped
¼ cup green olives, pitted and chopped
½ pound zucchini, sliced
1 tablespoon red pepper flakes

2 teaspoons dried oregano
½ cup white wine or vegetable broth
1 pound heirloom tomatoes, chopped
2 teaspoons sea salt
1 teaspoon black pepper
1 cup quark or sour cream
1 pound penne pasta, cooked al dente

Sauté the garlic and shallot in the olive oil until the shallot is soft and translucent. Add the capers, kalamata and green olives, zucchini, red pepper flakes, and oregano. Slowly add the wine or broth. Turn down the heat and simmer until the mixture is reduced by half. Add the tomatoes, salt, and pepper and let simmer for 10 minutes. Add the quark and remove from the heat. Toss with the cooked penne pasta.

. . . .

MY MATCH TO SEAN'S CHALLENGE gets its similarity in the first three letters: q-u-a. Quark is my substitute for Sean's quail. With the exception of my creamy additive and Sean's little fishies, our sauces are nearly identical. Quark is similar to crème fraîche and is popular in European countries. Its flavor can be best compared to sour cream yet with a milder taste and richer texture. It turns this typical robust red sauce into a softer pink puttanesca.

Sean

Avocado Swiss Chicken

Four 8-ounce boneless chicken breasts
2 Mexican avocados, sliced
2 Roma tomatoes, sliced thin
1 tablespoon garlic powder
2 tablespoons chopped fresh cilantro
1 cup white wine

Juice of 1 lime
8 slices baby Swiss cheese
1 teaspoon kosher salt
Pepper to taste
1 teaspoon paprika

Preheat the oven to 375 degrees. On a clean workspace, slice each chicken breast near the bottom but be careful not to cut all the way through. Turn the chicken breast 180 degrees to the right and make another slice near the top, also being careful not to cut all the way through. In both slits layer the avocados, tomatoes, garlic powder, and cilantro. Arrange the stuffed breasts in a 9 × 13 casserole and pour in the wine. Drizzle the lime juice over the top of the chicken; cover each breast with two slices of cheese and sprinkle with the salt, pepper, and paprika. Cover with foil and bake for 30 minutes. Uncover and bake for another 15 minutes or until the cheese is brown and bubbly. Carefully remove the chicken breasts from the casserole and use a little of the pan drippings for a sauce. Serve hot and enjoy.

• •

THE STUFFING METHOD USED IN THIS DISH is one of my favorites. It produces a layered effect that adds to the overall presentation. The beauty, however, is not just in the sight but in the taste as well. With subtle bites of Swiss and avocado this dish would be great with a glass of sauvignon blanc and a summer's rain.

I love that Maggie decided to throw down the cactus on this one. I think it shows great moxie.

Avocado Queso Cactus

Pico de Gallo

4 heirloom tomatoes, chopped
6 chopped scallions, white and light green parts only
1 minced onion

1 cup chopped cilantro
1 or 2 jalapeños, seeded and minced
Juice of 1 lime
1 teaspoon sea salt

In a bowl combine the tomatoes, scallions, onion, cilantro, jalapeño, lime juice, and sea salt and set aside to marinate.

Cactus

8 prickly pear cactus paddles
2 cups all-purpose organic flour
¼ cup garlic powder
¼ cup paprika
1 tablespoon sea salt

4 eggs, beaten
4 cups tortilla chips, crushed to a fine powder
4 cups queso fresco cheese
4 avocados, sliced

With a sharp knife, shave off the thorns from both sides of the cactus paddles. Trim off 1 inch on the base and ¼ inch around the outer edges. Rinse and pat dry. Set aside.

Sift together the flour, garlic powder, paprika, and sea salt onto a large plate or shallow dish. Put the beaten eggs in a separate shallow dish. Put crushed tortilla chips in another separate plate or shallow dish. Dredge the cactus in the flour mixture, shaking off the excess, then dip it into the egg. Coat thoroughly with crushed tortilla chips. Place coated cactus paddles on a large baking sheet (or sheets). Bake at 350 degrees for 30 minutes until the paddles are golden and crispy. Remove from the oven and place ½ cup cheese on each cactus paddle. Return to the oven and bake for another 5 minutes or until the cheese is golden and bubbly. Top each paddle with pico de gallo and avocado slices.

· ·

SIMILAR TO OKRA IN TEXTURE, prickly pear cactus paddles have a slippery interior flesh surrounded by a firm exterior skin. The taste is also akin to okra. Choose firm, flat paddles that are blemish free. You can find them fresh at most Mexican and South American markets. Served side by side with Sean's dish, the two will not be similar in appearances but the flavors should please everyone at the table who's in the mood for Tex-Mex cuisine. The meat eaters are sure to be intrigued by this dish, since cactus paddles on the table are still a little unusual in most areas of the United States.

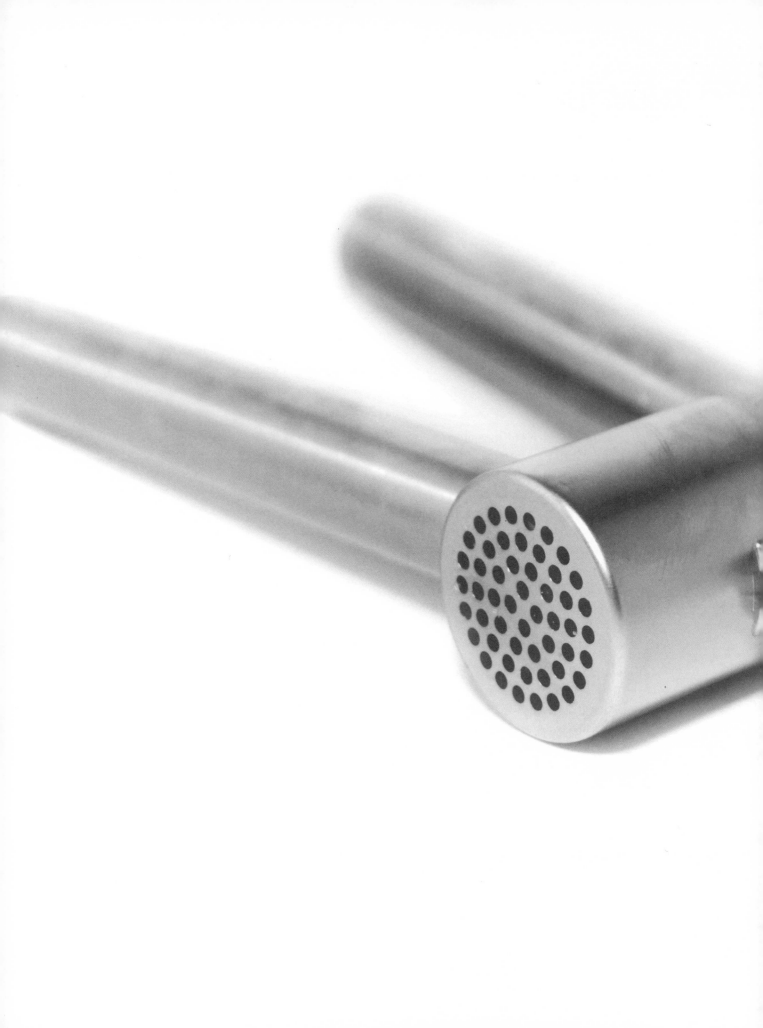

Fire

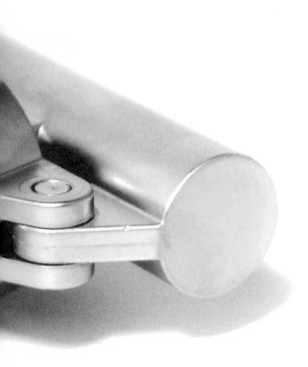

Sean

Roast Pork Tenderloin with Tomato-Jalapeño Confit

Tomato-Jalapeño Confit

5 whole Roma tomatoes
½ cup canned sliced jalapeño peppers, with ¼ cup juice reserved
3 garlic cloves
1 carrot, chopped

1 yellow onion, chopped
¼ cup red wine, any kind
3 tablespoons olive oil
Salt and pepper to taste

Combine all ingredients except reserved jalapeño juice in a small roasting pan and bake at 375 degrees until the top of the confit is black, about 40 minutes. Purée the baked mixture until smooth and strain. Serve warm on the side of the pork tenderloin.

Roast Pork Tenderloin

1 whole pork tenderloin, excess fat removed
2 tablespoons reserved canned jalapeño juice
2 garlic cloves, minced

1 tablespoon olive oil
Salt and pepper to taste

Preheat the oven to 375 degrees. Rub the pork tenderloin with the jalapeño juice, garlic, olive oil, salt, and pepper. Let stand in the refrigerator for 20 minutes. Bake, covered with foil, for 15 minutes, then bake uncovered for 10 minutes more. Remove the tenderloin from the oven and let it rest for 15 minutes before slicing and serving.

• •

THIS ONE GETS RIGHT IN THE BACK OF YOUR MOUTH. I promise that the juices will gush as this is being plated. The smoky heat from the confit empowers the indirect flavors of the pork. Settle this dish next to some buttered black-eyed peas and fried okra and prepare yourself for a repast worthy of remembering.

It is getting tiresome having to quaff the vegetarian's constant barrage of cholesterol and fat. The pork industry of today is completely unlike that of yesterday. No longer are they striving for the Hogzilla lard-producing porkers they once were. A much leaner, trimmer animal is the goal, one that contains less cholesterol than the shellfish vegetarians usually "cheat" with. Also, once cooked, the tenderloin is the least cholesterol-laden cut of meat. Once again, this bit of flesh will have gone through less toil, turmoil, and processing than that of any "mock meat."

The real atrocity is mock meatloaf. I have a theory, wild though it may be, that the bottled water companies, wanting to produce a higher demand for their product, created the mock meatloaf. What happens to your shredded documents when they've been recycled is what it should be called.

Neatloaf with Tomato-Dijon Sauce

1 slice toasted whole-wheat bread, finely diced
¼ cup toasted cashews
¼ cup toasted sunflower seeds
¼ cup toasted walnuts
2 tablespoons soy sauce
1 tablespoon nutritional yeast
1 cup vegetable broth
½ cup minced onion

1 tablespoon garlic, minced or pressed
½ cup chopped mushrooms
½ cup minced cauliflower
¼ cup grated carrot
1 teaspoon sea salt
1 teaspoon dried sage
1 teaspoon dried thyme

Place the toasted whole-wheat bread, cashews, sunflower seeds, and walnuts in the food processor and pulse to a coarse meal. Add the soy sauce, nutritional yeast powder, and half of the vegetable broth. With the remaining broth, sauté the onion, garlic, mushrooms, cauliflower, carrot, salt, sage, and thyme for 10 minutes or until the vegetables are softened. Add the mixture to the food processor and blend for another 3 to 5 minutes. Transfer to a well-oiled casserole and bake, covered, for 45 minutes.

Tomato-Dijon Sauce

4 tablespoons butter or margarine
4 tablespoons organic unbleached white flour
1 cup organic milk or soy milk
¼ cup Dijon mustard

2 cups chopped tomatoes
1 tablespoon finely chopped fresh basil
Sea salt and pepper to taste

Melt the butter in a saucepan. Add the flour a little at a time, stirring constantly to avoid lumps. Continue to cook until the butter and flour mixture is golden. Gradually add the milk until the sauce has thickened. Add the Dijon mustard, tomatoes, and basil. Season with the salt and pepper.

• •

THIS MOCK MEATLOAF IS THE CLOSEST MATCH I could think of for a pork tenderloin pairing. It is served in slices with a sauce, so in appearance it suits the carnivore's counterpart. Vegetarians can enjoy a dish packed with protein and B vitamins, the nutritional equivalent to the meat dish without all the fat or any of the cholesterol.

Sean

A Fine Duck Breast Grill

4 boneless Long Island duck breasts, with skin intact and fat trimmed
2 red onions, sliced into rings

1 large yellow squash, sliced lengthwise
1 large zucchini, cut diagonally
2 fennel bulbs, sliced

Score the duck by cutting into the skin on the diagonal, but be careful not to cut too deep. Turn the breast and score the skin again on the diagonal, creating a crosshatch appearance. On a grill over 3-second heat, start cooking the breast, skin side down. As the fat renders, it will drip onto the coals and cause flame bursts. Be careful that this doesn't overcook the breast. When the skin is golden and crispy, after about 3 minutes, turn the breast over and cook to a doneness of medium rare. Spray the sliced onions, squash, zucchini, and fennel lightly with the olive oil and season with salt and pepper. Grill the vegetables until tender. Divide the cooked vegetables between four plates, heaping them in the center. Slice the grilled duck breast on the bias and fan the slices around the heap of vegetables. Enjoy.

● ●

THIS IS ONE OF THOSE EYES-ROLLED-BACK DISHES. The red, buttery richness of the duck will put you in a trance of ecstasy. Don't be surprised if you hear Diana Krall singing "Can I Thank You in Advance" somewhere off in the distance. If you happen to be preparing this dish when Maggie is around, be sure to remove the grill grate after cooking your fine duck and sandblast the bejeezus out of it before you grill her veggies. Goodness knows her veggies can't be grilled where meat has been. Maybe you could offer her a bowl of granola and a napkin for the dribble she's generating as she looks at your plate.

A Fine Brie Baguette Grill

4 demi-baguettes (6 inches long), cut in half lengthwise
2 tablespoons butter
1 tablespoon olive oil
1 red onion, sliced thin

1 zucchini or yellow squash, cut in strips
1 red bell pepper, cut in strips
1 portobello mushroom, cut in strips
8 ounces firm brie cheese, cut in ½-inch strips

Heat the grill. Spread butter on both sides of each baguette half and set aside. Brush the cut-to-grill onion, squash, bell pepper, and mushroom with the olive oil and grill until tender and slightly charred. Layer the brie cheese and the grilled veg-etables on half of the buttered baguette. Top with the other buttered half and grill on low heat until the cheese starts to melt. Flip over and grill the other side.

. . . .

SEAN GAVE ME THE DUCK BREAST CHALLENGE and at first I thought it would be easy enough to substitute a tofu or tempeh filet for the flesh of the little bird's chest. But that wouldn't be much of a creative challenge. So instead I went a completely dif-ferent direction and put a fine twist on a classic, the grilled cheese sandwich. I stay with Sean's recipe by using all his vegetable accompaniments, piling them on the oozy melt of French heaven. I must say that the vegetables he uses for his feathered friend pair quite well with the brie.

Sean

Red Eye Ribeye

Four 10-ounce ribeye steaks
1 Vidalia onion, sliced
1 tablespoon olive oil
6 large button mushrooms, sliced

½ cup red wine
1 tablespoon butter
Pinch kosher salt

Beef Rub

½ cup ground French roast espresso coffee
   beans
¼ cup freshly ground black peppercorns
½ teaspoon freshly ground allspice

¼ teaspoon freshly ground cinnamon
½ teaspoon freshly ground nutmeg
¼ teaspoon freshly ground cloves
1 tablespoon kosher salt

Heat the grill to a 3-second heat. In a pan combine the ground coffee beans, ground peppercorns, allspice, cinnamon, nutmeg, cloves, and salt for the rub. Dredge the steaks in the rub, coating both sides thoroughly. Grill the steaks to the preferred doneness.

In a sauté pan over a high heat, sauté the onion in the olive oil. As it starts to turn translucent, add the mushrooms and deglaze with half of the wine. Continue to sauté the onion and mushrooms until the wine has reduced to almost nothing. Again deglaze with the remaining wine, add the salt, and reduce the liquid to almost nothing. Take the pan off the heat and stir in the butter. Pour the warm sauce over the grilled steaks and enjoy.

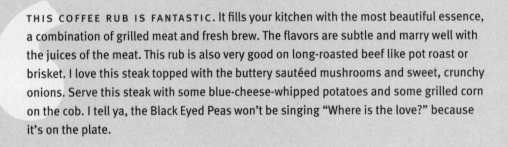

THIS COFFEE RUB IS FANTASTIC. It fills your kitchen with the most beautiful essence, a combination of grilled meat and fresh brew. The flavors are subtle and marry well with the juices of the meat. This rub is also very good on long-roasted beef like pot roast or brisket. I love this steak topped with the buttery sautéed mushrooms and sweet, crunchy onions. Serve this steak with some blue-cheese-whipped potatoes and some grilled corn on the cob. I tell ya, the Black Eyed Peas won't be singing "Where is the love?" because it's on the plate.

French Roast Lentils

1 tablespoon olive oil
2 Vidalia onions, sliced
2 carrots, finely diced
2 celery stalks, finely diced
6 mushrooms, sliced
1 teaspoon sea salt
½ cup red wine
4 cups French green lentils
8 cups water with 1 tablespoon sea salt added
2 tablespoons instant espresso coffee granules

1 teaspoon black pepper
½ teaspoon allspice
½ teaspoon nutmeg
¼ teaspoon cinnamon
¼ teaspoon cloves
1 bay leaf
½ cup minced fresh parsley
1 pound fresh spinach leaves
1 cup (8 ounces) crumbled feta cheese

Heat the olive oil and sauté the onions, carrots, celery, mushrooms, and salt until the onions are translucent. Add the red wine and continue to sauté until the wine evaporates. Add the lentils, water, espresso granules, black pepper, allspice, nutmeg, cinnamon, cloves, and bay leaf in a pot and bring to a boil. Reduce the heat and simmer for 30 to 40 minutes or until the lentils are just tender. Remove from the heat and stir in the parsley, spinach, and feta cheese. Serve warm with crusty French bread.

. . . .

THIS WAS A TRICKY MATCH. Trying to find a vegetarian pairing with coffee took a little time to figure out. I couldn't think of any vegetable that would welcome the dark aroma of coffee. I had to step out of the vegetable realm and into the world of legumes, where I stood a better chance of finding a suitable mate. The relaxed flavor of the lentils is amazing with a little perk of caffeine. The subtle coffee flavor gives a whole other dimension of intrigue and mystery to the otherwise humble lentil.

Sean

Glorious Gumbo

3 quarts chicken stock

3 large chicken thighs

2 tablespoons Worcestershire sauce

4 teaspoons Cajun or Creole seasoning

1½ teaspoons hot sauce

1 teaspoon garlic powder

1 teaspoon onion powder

1 tablespoon olive oil

1 cup coarsely chopped onion

½ cup coarsely chopped celery

½ cup coarsely chopped bell pepper

½ cup chopped fresh okra

2 tablespoons minced fresh garlic

1½ cups dark roux

1 bay leaf

1 pound andouille sausage, chopped

¼ teaspoon kosher salt

½ pound fresh shucked oysters

1 pound fresh 21/25 shrimp, peeled and deveined

¼ cup thinly sliced scallions

¼ cup minced fresh parsley

8 cups cooked rice

In a large pot, bring the chicken stock to a boil. Season the chicken thighs with the Worcestershire sauce, 3 teaspoons of the Cajun seasoning, 1 teaspoon of the hot sauce, garlic powder, and onion powder. Add the chicken and return to a boil. Lower the heat and simmer for 30 minutes. Strain the chicken, reserving the broth. Debone the chicken, discarding bones and skin. Coarsely chop the chicken and set aside.

In a large saucepot, heat the olive oil and add the onion, celery, bell pepper, okra, and garlic. Cook for 2 minutes. Add the roux, remaining hot sauce, remaining Creole seasoning, bay leaf, and reserved chicken broth. Bring to a boil, lower the heat, and simmer for 30 minutes. Add the sausage and salt. Continue to simmer uncovered for 15 minutes. Add the coarsely chopped chicken along with the oysters and shrimp and cook for 15 additional minutes. Stir in the scallions and parsley. Serve over rice and cherish.

• •

TO MAKE THE DARK ROUX, combine equal parts all-purpose flour and melted butter in a heavy-bottomed saucepot. Stir the mixture continuously as you cook it over medium to high heat, being careful not to burn it, until the roux reaches a rich mahogany color.

Compassionate Gumbo

¼ cup olive oil
Two 8-ounce tempeh
1 pound thinly sliced seitan
2 tablespoons granulated garlic
1 tablespoon granulated onion
1 teaspoon dried thyme
1 teaspoon salt
1 teaspoon pepper
½ teaspoon cayenne pepper
1 stick (½ cup) butter or soy margarine

¼ cup all-purpose organic flour
2 cups hot vegetable broth
1 cup fresh okra
1 cup yellow summer squash
1 cup celery
1 cup red bell pepper
1 cup onion
12 whole heirloom cherry tomatoes
6 garlic cloves, minced or pressed
1 tablespoon filé powder

Preheat the oven to 400 degrees. Coat the tempeh and seitan with the olive oil. In a separate bowl, combine the garlic, onion, thyme, salt, black pepper, and cayenne pepper. Add the tempeh and seitan to the spice mixture and toss until thoroughly coated. Spread evenly on a baking sheet and bake 23 minutes or until well encrusted.

In a large stockpot melt the butter and add the flour, whisking constantly until smooth (no lumps!). Continue whisking the roux until the color deepens to a dark brown and you smell a nice nutty aroma. Stir in half of the hot vegetable broth and the okra, squash, celery, bell pepper, onion, tomatoes, and garlic. Cook 15 minutes or more, stirring constantly until thickened. Add the remaining vegetable broth and the tempeh. Cover and simmer 30 minutes, stirring occasionally. Remove from the heat and add the filé powder. (Do not continue to cook after the filé powder is added or the dish will be stringy and gummy.)

· ·

WHO SAID GUMBO HAS TO BE A CARNIVORE'S CARNIVAL? This version of gumbo is less of a blood feast and more of a garden bounty. For a more regional flare, try using a variety of different vegetables seasonal to your area. Collard greens, kale, mustard greens, or spinach are a nice addition and are said to bring good luck. The filé powder is essential to the gumbo, but be mindful of its thickening properties. Once filé is added, immediately remove the pot from the heat and do not continue to cook as noted above in the recipe.

Sean

Blackened Beef Tournedos with Remoulade

4 beef tournedos (tenderloin cuts), about 1 inch thick and 2½ inches in diameter

4 strips of bacon
8 ounces spring mix salad greens

Beef Rub

4 tablespoons garlic powder
4 tablespoons onion powder
4 tablespoons paprika
4 tablespoons freshly ground fennel seed
8 tablespoons dry mustard
2 tablespoons ground rosemary

2 tablespoons ground oregano
4 tablespoons ground basil
2 tablespoons ground thyme
4 tablespoons kosher salt
8 tablespoons freshly ground black pepper

Wrap each tournedo with a strip of bacon, securing the bacon with a toothpick. Combine all rub ingredients and mix thoroughly. Dredge the tournedos in the rub, being sure to coat them evenly. In a very hot cast-iron skillet, sear the meat for 2 minutes on each side. Cover and cook for an additional 3 minutes.

Divide the spring mix between four plates, top with the blackened steaks, garnish with remoulade, and enjoy.

Remoulade

½ cup mayonnaise
2 tablespoons freshly squeezed lemon juice
1 tablespoon capers
1 tablespoon chopped gherkins

1 tablespoon Dijon mustard
1 anchovy fillet, minced
1 tablespoon finely chopped fresh parsley
½ teaspoon paprika

Combine all ingredients in a bowl and mix thoroughly. The remoulade can be kept in the refrigerator for 1 week.

• •

I LOVE THE FLAVOR COMBINATION OF THIS SMOKY, fiery, yummy rub and the creamy sweetness of the remoulade. Generally I pair this taste sensation with catfish, but I wanted my counterpart to Maggie's Butternut Medallions it to be a bit more carnivorous, so I chose the Beef Tournedos. And when the person next to you asks why the dish is named after a destructive funnel cloud, you can explain that it is pronounced "TOOR-nih-doh" and let them get back their squash.

The key to this dish is to get the skillet very, very hot. It will be rather smoky when you put the beef on so you might want to take the batteries out of the fire alarm and open the kitchen window, just until after dinner. But everybody in the neighborhood will want to know what that wonderful smell is and how they can get a bite.

These recipes side by side will make a very dramatic presentation on a combined vegetarians' and meat eaters' table. The meat eaters can enjoy the flavor combinations that Maggie has put together, though I doubt the vegetarians will admit to the Pavlovian desire they feel when they get a small whiff of the absolute bliss nestled on your plate.

Blackened Butternut Medallions with Feta Cheese

1 large (long-necked) butternut squash
1 cup flour
4 eggs, beaten

2 cups crumbled feta cheese
1 cup finely chopped fresh parsley

Blackening Rub

½ cup paprika
½ cup garlic powder
¼ cup black pepper
¼ cup onion powder
¼ cup dried oregano

¼ cup cayenne pepper
¼ cup dried thyme
2 tablespoons dried basil
2 tablespoons sea salt

Preheat the oven to 400 degrees. In a shallow dish, combine all the ingredients for the rub. Remove the stem and ¼ inch off the top of the squash. Cut the neck of the squash crosswise in ½-inch disks until you reach the cavity. Dip the squash disks into the flour and shake off the excess. Dip floured disks into the eggs and coat generously. Dip egg-coated disks into the rub and coat generously. Place the rub-coated disks on a well-oiled baking sheet. Bake for 15 minutes. Flip the squash disks over and bake for another 15 minutes or until tender.

In a small bowl combine the feta cheese and parsley. Remove the squash from the oven and top with feta and parsley mixture. Return to the oven for 5 to 10 minutes or until the cheese is golden.

. . . .

I GLADLY TAKE ON SEAN'S CHALLENGE with this low-fat, high-flavor dish. Like most of his meaty creations, the tenderloin cuts are too heavy to rise to the occasion. I chose to bake the squash medallions instead of frying 'em in a skillet for two reasons: first, to create an oil-free, lower-calorie version, and second, to avoid evacuating the house from the blackening cayenne fumes produced by pan searing. I think both our garnishes go well with the dish they are paired with. The light, tangy feta and fresh parsley accent the spicy, sweet butternut flesh. And of course Sean's artery-clogging mayonnaise pairs perfectly with the heavy red meat wrapped in fatty bacon. The visual presentation when serving these dishes side by side at the vegetarian-carnivore table will be dramatic, and so will the finish when the diners push away from the table. That's when you see the energy levels of those meat eaters plummet to near comatose while the squash diners are putting on some dancing tunes and hitting the dance floor with their happy, satisfied bellies.

Afterword

Sean

In the short time I've been on this blue dot I've come to discover that the middle path is the best. From what I've seen, those that go to extremes in excess or denial actually seclude themselves from the happiness and balance they are trying to achieve. In the world today, too many people are on too many diets that deny them too many things. In truth, your body, not your brain, tells you what you need. If your body is saying eat meat, don't deny it.

Our book. Is it the tome to last the ages we set out to create? It is what it is and only time will tell. I learned a long time ago how hard it is to translate works from the mind's eye to paper, plate, or canvas, though that's never stopped me from trying. I'm proud of what we accomplished, Maggie and I. We had fun and amazingly have stayed friends. I hold that friendship dear and hope that it, as well as the debate, lasts as long as we have the urge to eat.

Maggie

Now that Sean and I have had our culinary bout, I feel we have come to an agreement. We both agree that our recipes are better than the other's. He still thinks my recipes are incomplete without the meat and I stand firm in my vegetarian convictions. Being given a recipe to tweak to our own tastes has been a creative challenge. Each of us designed our dishes to match up to the other's in nearly all aspects but that one main component. And that centerpiece is still as contentious as it was in the beginning. Neither of us has converted the other. Thank goodness. The friendship we have is that of one great delicious debate.

Weights and Measures

Approximate Metric Equivalents

A pint is a pound the whole world round with water, milk, and eggs.

Volume

U.S. SYSTEM	METRIC EQUIVALENT
¼ teaspoon	1 milliliter (mL)
½ teaspoon	2.5 mL
¾ teaspoon	4 mL
1 teaspoon	5 mL
1¼ teaspoons	6 mL
1½ teaspoons	7.5 mL
1¾ teaspoons	8.5 mL
2 teaspoons	10 mL
1 tablespoon	15 mL
2 tablespoons	30 mL
¼ cup (2 ounces)	59 mL
B/d cup	79 mL
½ cup (4 ounces)	118 mL
C/d cup	158 mL
¾ cup (6 ounces)	178 mL
1 cup (8 ounces)	237 mL
1½ cups (12 ounces)	355 mL
1 pint (2 cups/16 ounces)	473 mL
3 cups (18 ounces)	710 mL
4 cups (1 quart)	.95 liter (L)
1.06 quarts	1 L
4 quarts (1 gallon)	3.8 L

Weight

U.S.A.	METRIC
.035 ounce	1 gram (g)
¼ ounce	7 g
½ ounce	14 g
¾ ounce	21 g
1 ounce	28 g
1½ ounces	42.5 g
2 ounces	57 g
3 ounces	85 g
4 ounces	113 g
5 ounces	142 g
6 ounces	170 g
7 ounces	198 g
8 ounces	454 g
16 ounces (1 pound)	454 g
2.2 pounds	1 kilogram

Index

aioli, 19, 76
alfalfa sprouts, 12
almonds, 86
anchovy fillets, 35, 90, 104
andouille sausage, 102
Apple-Brined Chops, 62
apple chutney, 63
apples, 54, 62, 63
artichoke hearts, 5, 61
Avgolemono Sauce, 73
avocado dishes
    Avocado Melt with Herb-Mus-
        tard Dressing, 12
    Avocado Queso Cactus, 93
    Avocado Swiss Chicken, 92
    Mole Marinated Tempeh with
        Strawberry Avocado Salsa,
        87
    Smoked Halibut on Ciabbata
        with Fried Avocado Slices
        and Roasted Yellow Pepper
        Crème Fraîche, 13

bacon, 5, 104
baguettes, 99
bain-marie, 6
    defined, 4
Balsamic Syrup, 72
barbecue sauce, blueberry, 64
Basil Oil, 72
beans
    black, 20, 36, 37, 40
    garbanzo, 18, 26
    Great Northern, 21, 67
    lentils, 101
    pinto, 21, 81
    white, 21
beef
    brisket, 64
    chuck roast, 47
    ground, 35, 37, 66
    pot roast, 68
    ribeye steaks, 100

    round steak, 51
    rub, 100, 104
    tenderloin fillets, 60
    tournedos, 104
Beef Brisket with Blueberry Barbe-
    cue Sauce, 64
Beef Stroganoff, 47
beer, 15, 68
bison, 9–10
Black Bean and Sweet Potato
        Cakes with Jalapeño-Chive
        Sour Cream, 40
black bean mojo, 36, 37
Blackened Beef Tournedos with
        Remoulade, 104
Blackened Butternut Medallions
        with Feta Cheese, 105
blackening rub, 105
blueberries, 64
blueberry barbecue sauce, 64
blue cheese, 48
Bolshevik Beet-n-Blue Gratin, 48
bread cubes, 5
breads
    breadcrumbs, 84
    buns, whole-grain, 65
    ciabbata, 13
    crusty, 68
    demi-baguettes, 99
    Italian, 73
    pita, 26
    whole-wheat, 97
brisket, 64
brown sugar, 64, 65
Brownville mills, 21
Bruschetta, 73
bulgur wheat, 18, 69

cactus paddles, prickly pear, 93
Cajun seasoning, 102
calamari, 23
capers, 13, 41, 67, 74, 85, 90, 91,
    104

The Carmichael, 60
cashews, 97
casseroles
    Beef Stroganoff, 87
    Bolshevik Beet-n-Blue Gratin,
        87
    Gardener's Pie, 87
    Jackfruit Zucchini Casserole, 87
    Shepherd's Pie with Welsh Rab-
        bit, 87
    Southwest Black Bean Casse-
        role, 20
    Turkey Zucchini Casserole, 87
    Wild Mushroom Seitan Stroga-
        noff, 87
caul fat, about, 31–32
cheese
    Asiago, 4
    baby Swiss, 92
    blue, 48
    brie, 99
    buffalo mozzarella, 75
    cheddar, 5, 12, 40, 68
    chèvre, 14, 49, 55, 84, 85
    cottage, 34, 35, 48
    cream cheese, 5
    feta, 23, 101, 105
    goat, 14
    Havarti, 7
    Manchego, 13
    mozzarella, 6, 12, 24, 35, 75
    Parmesan, 20, 34, 35, 42, 61
    Parmesan reggiano, 43
    provolone, 6, 12
    queso fesco, 93
    Stilton blue, 60
chicken, 5, 19, 25, 53
    breasts, 86, 92
    gizzards, 37
    livers, 37
    thighs, 102
chicken dishes
    Avocado Swiss Chicken, 92
    Eric-a-Strata, 5
    Garlic and Herb Roasted
        Chicken with Vegetables, 25
    Strawberry Marinated Chicken
        Breast with Mole, 86
    Tuesday Night Burger with Gin-
        ger-Lime Aioli, 19
chickpeas, 22

chili oil, 40
Chinese black rice, 79
chipotles, 64
chives, 7, 40, 47
chocolate, Mexican, 86
cholesterol, 4, 5
chutney, 54
    apple, 63
ciabbata, 13
cocoa powder, 64, 87
coconut milk, 30, 31, 52
coffee beans, French roast
    espresso, 100
coffee granules, instant espresso,
    101
compassion, xii
Compassionate Gumbo, 103
condiments, sambal oelek, 9
confit, 96
Cornbread Muffins, 81
cornichons, 15
Cornish game hens, 84
cornmeal, 40, 81
cottage cheese, 34, 35, 48
crème fraîche, 13
Creole seasoning, 102
crepe pans, 16
crepes
    Golden Crepes with Goat
        Cheese, Spinach, and Straw-
        berries, 14
    Mediatrice Crepes (Peacekeep-
        ing Crepes), 15
    Crustless Spinach and Mushroom
        Quiche, 6
currants, 54
Curried Egg-less Salad Wrap, 8
curries
    about, 30
    Curried Egg-less Salad Wrap, 8
    Spinach and Squash Chickpeas
        in Creamy Coconut Sauce, 30

daikons, 9
dairy products
    butter, 60, 97
    cottage cheese, 34, 35
    milk, 7, 14, 15, 42, 68
    quark, 91
    sour cream, 6, 13, 15, 46, 47, 50,
        61, 68, 81, 91

whipping cream, 15, 51, 74, 84,
    88
yogurt, 67
deglazing, 32
demi-baguettes, 99
dill fronds, 41
Dirty Rice Stuffed Peppers with
    Black Bean Mojo, 37
docking, 7
duck, 80, 98
Duck Breast Stuffed Trout, 80

egg dishes
    Crustless Spinach and Mush-
        room Quiche, 6
    Eric-a-Strata, 5
    Golden Crepes with Goat
        Cheese, Spinach, and Straw-
        berries, 14
    Lobster Quiche, 7
    Mediatrice Crepes (Peacekeep-
        ing Crepes), 15
    Roasted Fennel Frittata, 4
egg noodles, 46, 47
eggplant, 22, 23, 42, 66, 67, 75
Eggplant Boat on the Mediterra-
    nean, 22
eggs, 14, 15, 66, 67
    in casserole, 5
    for coating, 93, 105
    in frittata, 4
    poached, 73
    in quiche, 6, 7
Eric-a-Strata, 5

falafel, 18
Falafel Burger with Tahini-Mint
    Dressing, 18
farmers' markets, xii
fennel, 4. See also spices and
    herbs
Fig and Orzo Stuffed Acorn
    Squash, 85
figs, 85
    black mission, 84
    Calimyrna, 84
Fig Stuffed Game Hens, 84
filé powder, 103
A Fine Brie Baguette Grill, 99
A Fine Duck Breast Grill, 98
fish and seafood

calamari, 23
halibut, 78
halibut, smoked, 13
lobster, 7
oysters, 15, 102
salmon, 41, 49, 74
scallops, 23
shrimp, 23, 60, 102
talapia, 72
trout, 80
tuna, 49
tuna steaks, 76
five-spice powder, about, 63
flax seed, about, 40
Food Lover's Companion, 5
French Roast Lentils, 101
fresh food, xiii. *See also* farmers'
    markets
frittata, 4
fruit
    apples, 54, 62, 63
    blueberries, 64
    jackfruit, 65
    strawberries, 14, 86, 87

garam masala, 8
garbanzo beans, 18, 26
Gardener's Pie, 69
garlic, granulated, 103
Garlic and Herb Roasted Chicken
    with Vegetables, 25
Garlic and Herb Roasted Summer
    Vegetables with Fresh Moz-
    zarella, 24
gazpacho, 27
ghee, 52
gherkins, 104
Gingered Bison Lettuce Wraps
    with a Cold Ginger Sauce, 9
Glorious Gumbo, 102
G-Ma's Goulash, 51
Golden Crepes with Goat Cheese,
    Spinach, and Strawberries,
    14
goulash
    G-Ma's Goulash, 51
    Hungarian Tempeh Goulash, 50
grapefruit juice, 13
grape leaves, 80
gratin
    Bolshevik Beet-n-Blue Gratin, 48

greens, mustard, 49
Grilled Eggplant alla Caprese, 75
Grilled Halibut on Nutty Rice, 78
Grilled Salmon alla Piccata, 74
ground beef, 35, 37, 66
ground lamb, 66
ground pork, 35, 37
ground turkey, 88
gumbos
    Compassionate Gumbo, 103
    Glorious Gumbo, 102

halibut, 78
    smoked, 13
heirloom, defined, xii
herbs. *See* spices and herbs
hoisin sauce, 9
honey, 9, 31, 52, 73, 78, 84
Honeydew Prawns with Chickpea
    Gazpacho Served in a Chilled
    Melon Bowl, 27
horseradish, 21, 54, 63
hot sauce, 102
hummus, 26
Hungarian Tempeh Goulash, 50

jackfruit, about, 65, 89
Jackfruit Pineapple Barbecue on a
    Bun, 65
Jackfruit Zucchini Casserole, 89
James Arthur Vineyards, 21
Jitterbug Perfume (Robbins), 54
julienne, 10

lasagna, 34
Lasagna the Right Way, 35
lavender oil, 49
lemon, 25
lentils, French green, 101
lettuce, 8
    romaine, 9
liqueur, Midori, 27
liquid smoke, 65
lobster, 7
Lobster Quiche, 7
Long Island duck breasts, 98
Love Boat del Mar, 23

mayonnaise, 12, 41, 104
    jalapeño-mint, 41
meat

beef: brisket, 64; chuck roast,
    47; ground, 35, 37, 66; pot
    roast, 68; ribeye steaks, 100;
    round steak, 51; tenderloins,
    60; tournedos, 104
bison, 9
chicken, 5, 19, 25, 37
mutton, ground lamb, 66
pork: andouille sausage, 102;
    bacon, 5, 19, 104; chops, 62;
    ground, 35, 37; tenderloin,
    96
poultry: capons, 31; chicken, 53,
    86, 92, 102; Cornish game
    hens, 84; duck, 80, 98; os-
    trich, 55; quail, 90; turkey,
    ground, 88
veal, 43
meatloaf, mock
    Neatloaf with Tomato-Dijon
    Sauce, 97
Mediatrice Crepes (Peacekeeping
    Crepes), 15
melons, honeydew, 27
Midori liqueur, 27
milk, 7, 14, 15, 42
mint, 18, 19, 25
mirin, 77
mojo, black bean, 36, 37
molasses, 9, 19, 62, 63, 90
mole, 86, 87
Mole Marinated Tempeh with
    Strawberry Avocado Salsa,
    87
Moussaka Mollie, 67
Moussaka Rocka, 66
mung bean sprouts, 13
mushrooms, 6, 66, 69, 74, 97, 101
    button, 46, 100
    crimini, 47
    morel, 47
    porcini, 46, 47
    portobello, 46, 61, 67, 99
mustard, 12, 64
    Dijon, 47, 48, 97, 104
    dry, 43, 49, 104
    greens, 49
    whole-grain, 55
mutton, ground lamb, 66

Nayonnaise, 8

Neatloaf with Tomato-Dijon Sauce, 97
Nebraska White Beans and Rice, 21
nori seaweed, 77, 79
nuts
    almonds, 86
    cashews, 97
    peanuts, 78
    pine, 14, 66
    pistachios, 49
    walnuts, 48, 61, 85, 97
Nutty Rice, 78

olive oil, about, 24
olives
    green, 90, 91
    kalamata, 22, 23, 90, 91
Omaha Steaks, 60
onion powder, 47
onions, Vidalia, 84, 85, 100, 101
orange juice, 64
oregano, 24
organic food, xiii
orzo paste, 85
ostrich, about, 55
Ostrich Filets with Roasted Beet Relish, 55
ouzo, 23
oysters, 102
    about, 15

pancetta, 35
Pan-Fried Tofu with Silken Wasabi Sauce, 77
panko, 13, 41, 43, 84, 89
Pan-Seared Tuna with Wasabi Aioli, 76
pasta
    egg noodles, 46
    lasagna, 34, 35
    penne, 90, 91
pasta dishes
    Lasagna the Right Way, 35
    Penne Puttanesca with Quark, 91
    Penne Puttanesca with Roasted Quail, 91
    Seasonal Lasagna, 34
peanut butter, 52, 53, 65
peanut sauce, 52

Penne Puttanesca with Quark, 91
Penne Puttanesca with Roasted Quail, 90
pepper, lack of, 5
peppercorns, 100
peppers
    bell, 13, 20, 22, 23, 24, 25, 27, 36, 37, 50, 52, 78, 79, 81, 99, 102, 103
    chili, 86
    chipotles, 64
    jalapeño, 20, 36, 40, 41, 79, 81, 93, 96
Pica de Gallo, 93
pie dough, 7
pine nuts, 14, 66
Pinto Vegetable Stuffed Cornbread, 81
pistachios, 49
pita, 26
Pleskac Portobello, 61
Poached Tofu, 73
pork
    andouille sausage, 102
    bacon, 5, 19, 104
    chops, 62
    ground, 35, 37
    tenderloin, 96
pork dishes
    Apple-Brined Chops, 62
    Dirty Rice Stuffed Peppers with Black Bean Mojo, 37
    Glorious Gumbo, 102
    Lasagna the Right Way, 35
    Roast Pork Tenderloin with Tomato-Jalapeño Confit, 96
    Tuesday Night Burger with Ginger-Lime Aioli, 19
potatoes
    new, 24
    parboiling, 5
    red, 25, 50, 68, 69
    Russian banana fingerling, 51
    sweet, 40
    Yukon Gold, 48, 50, 69
pot roast, leftover, 68
poultry
    capons, 31
    chicken, 53, 86, 92
    chicken thighs, 102
    duck, 80, 98

ostrich, 55
quail, 90
turkey, ground, 88
prawns, 27
pumpkin seeds, 36, 87
puttanesca, 90

quail, 90
quark, 91
quiche
    Crustless Spinach and Mushroom Quiche, 6
    Lobster Quiche, 7
quinoa, about, 36
Quinoa Stuffed Peppers with Black Bean Mojo, 36

radicchio, 49
raisins, 54, 63, 86
Red Eye Ribeye, 100
red peppers, roasted, 5
remoulade, 104
ribeye steaks, 100
rice, 21, 37, 102
    basmati, 30, 52
    brown, 78
    Chinese black, 79
    Golden, 52
rice wine vinegar, 27
roasted beet chutney, 54
roasted beet relish, 55
Roasted Fennel Frittata, 4
Roasted Quail, 90
roasting peppers, 13
Roast Pork Tenderloin with Tomato-Jalapeño Confit, 96
Robbins, Tom, 54
Rosowski, Jim, 88
Rosowski, Susan, 88
roux, 102, 103

Saffron Poached Tilapia Painted with Balsamic Syrup and Basil Oil, 72
Saffron Poached Tofu on Fennel Bruschetta with Avgolemono Sauce, 73
salad greens, 104
salmon, 41, 49, 74
Salmon and Tuna Carpaccio with Roasted Beets, 49

Salmon Cakes with Jalapeño-Mint Mayo, 41
salsa, 87
sambal oelek, 9
satay
    Seitan Satay over Golden Rice, 52
sausage, andouille, 102
scallions, 9, 27, 36, 37, 40, 41, 52, 79, 93, 102
scallops, 23
seafood. *See* fish and seafood
seasonal foods, 32
Seasonal Lasagna, 34
seasoning, Old Bay seasoning, 15
seitan (wheat gluten), xii, 46, 52, 103
Seitan Satay over Golden Rice, 52
Sesame Black Rice, 79
sesame oil, 52, 78, 79, 80
sesame seeds, 26, 52, 79, 86, 87
shallots, 7, 49, 90, 91
Shepherd's Pie with Welsh Rabbit, 68
sherry, 7, 22, 23, 46, 47
shrimp, 23, 60, 102
Silken Wasabi Sauce, 77
Smoked Halibut on Ciabbata with Fried Avocado Slices and Roasted Yellow Pepper Crème Fraîche, 13
sour cream, 13, 46, 47, 50, 68, 81, 91
    jalapeño-chive, 40
Southwest Black Bean Casserole, 20
soy margarine, 103
soy-meat substitutes, xi
soy milk, 69, 81, 89, 97
spices and herbs
    allspice, 100, 101
    basil, 5, 6, 12, 13, 22, 23, 24, 25, 34, 35, 42, 43, 49, 52, 61, 72, 75, 88, 89, 90, 97, 104, 105
    bay leaves, 37, 46, 50, 51, 64, 101, 102
    caraway, 48, 50, 54
    cardamom, 8
    cayenne pepper, 26, 27, 30, 37, 53, 78, 103, 105
    chili powder, 64, 86, 87

chipotle pepper, 87
chipotle powder, 87
chives, 7, 40, 47
cilantro, 8, 9, 19, 20, 36, 41, 52, 79, 81, 87, 92, 93
cinnamon, 19, 30, 62, 86, 87, 100, 101
cloves, 86, 100, 101
coriander, 8, 14, 18, 20, 30, 36, 37, 52, 55, 86
cumin, 8, 14, 18, 19, 21, 23, 26, 30, 31, 36, 37, 40, 52, 64, 65, 81, 87
curry, 8
dill, 7, 12, 54
fennel, 7, 23, 25, 34, 43, 48, 61, 62, 73, 86, 88, 98, 104
fennel seeds, 34, 35
filé powder, 103
five-spice powder, 63
flax seed, 40
garam masala, 8
garlic powder, 47, 104, 105
garlic salt, 51
ginger, 8, 9, 19, 30, 31, 52, 53, 63
Hungarian paprika, 50, 51
Mexican oregano, 25
mint, 18, 19, 25
mustard, 21, 64
nutmeg, 6, 7, 15, 47, 67, 73, 100, 101
onion powder, 47, 104, 105
oregano, 22, 23, 24, 34, 35, 36, 37, 40, 42, 64, 88, 89, 91, 104, 105
paprika, 19, 65, 92, 93, 104, 105
parsley, 4, 6, 34, 35, 46, 48, 66, 67, 69, 85, 101, 102, 104, 105
rosemary, 24, 42, 46, 104
saffron, 72, 73
saffron, about, 72
sage, 21, 25, 31, 68, 97
savory, 47, 84
tarragon, 40
thyme, 12, 21, 24, 25, 47, 65, 69, 80, 81, 97, 103, 104, 105
tumeric, 8, 14, 18, 23, 30, 31, 52, 73
Spicy Hummus Stuffed Pita, 26
Spinach and Squash Chickpeas in Creamy Coconut Sauce, 30

Spinach and Squash Stuffed Capon Poached in Coconut Milk, 31
sprouts
    alfalfa, 12, 26
    mung bean, 13
steak, 60
    ribeye, 100
strata, 4
strawberries, 14, 86, 87
Strawberry Marinated Chicken Breast with Mole, 86
stroganoff, 46
sugar, brown, 64, 65
sunflower seeds, 12, 97
Swiss chard, 41, 80, 81

tahini, 18, 26
tempeh (soy), xii, 50, 54, 63, 87, 103
Tempeh Chop with Apple Chutney, 63
Tempeh Filets with Roasted Beet Chutney, 54
Tiga-Dega-Na, 53
tofu, xii, 8, 52, 73, 77, 79
Tofu Ceviche on Sesame Black Rice, 79
tomatoes, 19, 35, 51, 53, 86, 87, 90, 97
    balsamic marinated, 34
    beefsteak, 15
    heirloom, 8, 12, 18, 20, 22, 24, 26, 34, 67, 75, 81, 91, 93
    heirloom cherry, 103
    plum, 27
    Roma, 23, 42, 92, 96
    sun-dried, 36
Tomato Jalapeño Confit, 96
tomato juice, 27
Tomato Mustard Sauce, 97
tomato paste, 27, 35, 53, 86
tomato purée, 66
tomato sauce, 36, 37, 50, 64, 65
tortilla chips, 93
tortillas, 8, 20
trout, 80
truffle oil, 15, 46, 61
Tuesday Night Burger with Ginger-Lime Aioli, 19
tumeric, 8, 14, 18, 23, 30, 31, 52, 73

tuna, 49
tuna steaks, 76
turkey, brining, 62
Turkey Zucchini Casserole, 88

Veal Parmesan, 43
vegetables
  beets: baby, 49; chioggia, 48,
    49, 54; red, 48, 54, 55
  broccoli, 52
  brussels sprouts, 25
  cabbage, white, 9
  carrots, 9, 22, 25, 26, 50, 51, 68,
    69, 79, 96, 97, 101
  cauliflower, 97
  celery, 21, 25, 27, 37, 50, 79, 101,
    102, 103
  chickpeas, 27, 30
  corn, 81
  cucumbers, 9, 18, 19, 26, 27
  eggplant, 66, 75
  leeks, 46
  mustard greens, 49
  okra, 102, 103
  okra pods, 53, 102
  peas, 68, 69
  pinto beans, 81
  spinach, 6, 14, 15, 30, 31, 61,
    101
  squash, 98, 99, 105; acorn, 85;
    butternut, 31, 105; crookneck,
    30; summer, 103; yellow, 98;
    yellow summer, 24
  sweet peas, 68
  sweet potatoes, 40
  Swiss chard, 41, 80, 81
  tarragon, 40
  tomatoes, 19, 35, 51, 53, 86, 87,
    90, 97; balsamic marinated,
    34; beefsteak, 15; heirloom,
    8, 12, 18, 20, 22, 24, 26, 34,
    67, 75, 81, 91, 93; heirloom
    cherry, 103; plum, 27; Roma,
    23, 42, 92, 96; sun-dried, 36
  turnips, 69; baby, 24
  yams, 53
  zucchinis, 24, 30, 53, 88, 89,
    90, 91, 98, 99
vinegar, 63, 87
  apple cider, 65
  balsamic, 22, 34, 72, 75, 78, 84

cane, 9, 49
  red wine, 54, 55
  rice wine, 27, 31, 78

Wahoo Locker, 21
walnuts, 48, 61, 85, 97
Wasabi Aioli, 76
wasabi paste, 76, 77
Wasabi Sauce, 77
Welsh Rabbit, 68
whipping cream, 74, 84, 88
White Eggplant Parmesan, 42
white sauce, 42
Wild Mushroom Seitan Stroganoff,
  46
wine
  Chablis, 72
  port, 55, 84
  red, 35, 90, 96, 100, 101
  rice, 77
  sherry, 7, 22, 23, 46, 47
  white, 60, 74, 86, 88, 89, 90,
    91, 92
Worcestershire sauce, 66, 79, 102
  vegetarian, 63, 65

yeast, nutritional, 69, 89, 97
yogurt, 67

Illustration Credits

All photos © iStockphoto.com:

Andrea Gingerich: two whisks
Mike Brittain: measuring cups
Eric Etman: salt and pepper shakers
Bradley Mason: fork and knife
Westmacott Photography:
  vegetable peeler
Steve Jacobs: metal colander
John Sigler: grater/microplane
Yin Yang: juicer
Ljupco Smokovski: potato masher

Chris Hill: frying pan
Chris Hill: stock pot
UteHill: single whisk
Monolinea: cleaver
Bill Noll: spatula
Bas Evers: slotted spoon
Camp Spot: egg separator
Marko Roeper: garlic press
Igor Kisselev: wooden fork
  and spoon

In the At Table series

Spiced
Recipes from Le Pré Verre
Philippe Delacourcelle
Translated and with a preface by Adele King
and Bruce King

Eating in Eden
Food and American Utopias
Edited by Etta M. Madden and Martha L. Finch

Recovering Our Ancestors' Gardens
Indigenous Recipes and Guide to Diet
and Fitness
Devon Abbott Mihesuah

Dueling Chefs
A Vegetarian and a Meat Lover Debate the Plate
Maggie Pleskac and Sean Carmichael

A Taste of Heritage
Crow Indian Recipes and Herbal Medicines
Alma Hogan Snell
Edited by Lisa Castle

Available in Bison Books Editions

The Food and Cooking of Eastern Europe
Lesley Chamberlain
With a new introduction by the author

The Food and Cooking of Russia
Lesley Chamberlain
With a new introduction by the author

The World on a Plate
A Tour through the History of America's
Ethnic Cuisine
Joel Denker

Masters of American Cookery
M. F. K. Fisher, James Beard,
Craig Claiborne, Julia Child
Betty Fussell
With a preface by the author

Good Things
Jane Grigson

Jane Grigson's Fruit Book
Jane Grigson
New introduction by Sara Dickerman

Jane Grigson's Vegetable Book
Jane Grigson
New introduction by Amy Sherman

Dining with Marcel Proust
A Practical Guide to French Cuisine
of the Belle Epoque
Shirley King
Foreword by James Beard

Pampille's Table
Recipes and Writings from the French
Countryside from Marthe Daudet's Les Bons
Plats de France
Translated and adapted by Shirley King

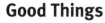